INDIAN DEMOCRACY

An Uneven Path

S.K. Narang

INDIA • SINGAPORE • MALAYSIA

ISBN 979-8-88783-346-0

CONTENTS

CONTENTS

"Constitutional morality is not a natural sentiment. It has to be cultivated. We must realise that people have yet to learn it. Democracy in India is only a top dressing on an Indian soil, which is essentially undemocratic."

– BR Ambedkar

PART – A

1

IN SEARCH OF PATH

The origin of democracy is obscure and shrouded in mystery. Some historians trace its origin to the late Bronze Age Civilisation (1500 BC–1200 BC) and believe that it started from contemporary Syria, Iraq and Iran region from where it moved to the Indian subcontinent. Republics, governed by assemblies, were established in wider regions of India in early Vedic period around 1500 BC and in the West of Indian subcontinent during the 5th century BC. Another set of historians believe that democracy originated around 550 BC among the Greeks in a small Mediterranean city of Athens on account of the outbreak of violence, murders, uprising and power grabbing. Cleirthenes, an aristocrat, realised that a long-lasting system of government could not survive on tyranny and violence, and that a permanent system could only be based on the principle of self-governance. The Greek called this system *demokratia,* coined from two words, *demos* meaning 'people' and *kratos* meaning 'power' or 'authority'. The word 'democracy', where power rests with the people, is believed to have been derived

9

from *demokratia*. Like other great scientific inventions and discoveries, democracy is one of the greatest social achievements of man. With passage of time and change of needs of society, democracy passed through various forms like 'assembly', 'liberal', 'social', 'republican' but the basic principles of 'self-governance', 'respect for human rights' and 'rule of law' remained unchanged.

Birth of modern democracy in the world is associated with French Revolution of 1789 also caused by tyranny, violence and political crisis that resulted in the end of a cruel regime in France. Ideas of thinkers and philosophers like Descartes, Lock and then Montesquieu, Voltaire and Rousseau greatly inspired the people. Monarchy was no longer seen as divine ordained and monarch Louis XVI was condemned to death. French Revolution gave the world three immortal slogans of Liberty, Equality and Fraternity that became the basis of all democracies and their constitutions.

Today, democracy is the most powerful social force that has magnetised the people all over the globe. We have now over 120 countries following representative democracy, India being the largest. In most of the countries, democracy has been the product and outcome of revolutions and violence. In India, the land of peace and non-violence, its birth was through a democratic process and through well-intentioned thoughts and discussions.

Democracy in India was born on 26th January 1950 though the real struggle goes much before this. Immediately after the First War of Independence in 1857, the freedom movement picked up and gained strength with the birth of Congress in 1885. The Congress started with the demand of Home Rule which grew into complete independence. The nefarious design of 'divide-and-rule' of the British resulted in partition and India got independence on 15th August, 1947. On that memorable eve, Jawaharlal Nehru, the first Prime Minister of India, remarked, "A moment comes, which comes but rarely in history, when we step out from the old to the new". With humility he said, "the future is not one of ease or resting but of incessant striving…"

After independence, the primary task was to draft a constitution and lay path for Indian democracy. Bhimrao Ramji Ambedkar was appointed Chairman of the drafting committee. Born in a poor 'untouchable' family, he was a great intellectual, an eminent jurist and an admirable reformer. His contribution to the framing of a vibrant constitution is venerable.

The founding fathers of the Constitution were leaders of great insight and scholarship and had shown considerable wisdom in drafting the same by making it all inclusive. They were clear of the path of democracy and the direction in which the country should proceed. It took them three years to put the Constitution together and finally laid down a parliamentary form of democracy.

Indian Constitution, the largest in the world, begins with words:

"WE, THE PEOPLE OF INDIA, having solemnly resolved to constitute India into a SOVEREIGN SOCIALIST SECULAR DEMOCRATIC REPUBLIC and to secure to all its citizens:

JUSTICE, social, economic and political;

LIBERTY of thought, expression, belief, faith and worship;

EQUALITY of status and opportunity;

and to promote among them all

FRATERNITY ensuring the dignity of the individual and the unity and integrity of the Nation;"

The words 'democratic republic' succinctly laid the path of our democracy. Strictly speaking republic and democracy don't mean the same. India is a republic for it is 'Union of States'.

Indian Constitution guarantees fundamental rights to ensure justice, equality and liberty. It is based on four fundamental principles - individual liberty, faith equality, gender equality and economic equality. All civilised countries also practice equality before law though no society is or has ever been truly equal as equality is an ever-elusive aspiration. Still it is essential for every society to strive for equality of status and opportunity for the healthy growth and survival of democracy. Eradication of social injustice and providing universal adult franchise were its other basic principles. According to Ambedkar, Indian Constitution, the soul of democracy, is not merely a charter of rights but also a vehicle of social empowerment. All this can work as long as the people and the polity are accountable not only towards their rights but also towards their obligations and duties.

Based on centuries of Indian customs and traditions, the framers wanted all religions to be treated equally. Time has paid rich dividend regarding this trust in the wisdom of the framers. At the time of its adoption, the Constitution neither declared any state religion nor proclaimed India a secular state. Twenty-six years after promulgation, the Preamble was amended to include the word 'secular'. However, India was 'secular' even without a formal declaration as 'equality before law and equal protection of laws' as fundamental rights mandated the state not to discriminate on grounds of religion, race, caste, sex or place of birth.

Flexibility is one of the greatest strengths of Indian Constitution. Framers were acutely aware that for its survival a constitution must be able to adapt with the changing times. They displayed great foresight while drafting the amendment provisions and wanted it to be neither too rigid nor too flexible. No provision of the Constitution was kept out of the reach of Parliament. Some provisions can be amended by simple majority in the Parliament, most by two-third majority, while some additionally require ratification by at least half the states of the union. Till January 2020 there have been 104 amendments to the Constitution that include amendments to Schedules, changes in Articles and insertion of new Articles. Despite several amendments it has stood the test of time.

Indian Constitution created several institutions like Election Commission (EC), Supreme Court (SC) and Comptroller and Auditor General (CAG) which are the saviour and protector of democracy. EC is an autonomous constitutional authority as per Article 324 of the Constitution and subsequently enacted 'The Representation of the People Act'. It is responsible for administering elections and ensures free and fair elections to allow people to fearlessly exercise their franchise. "In the discharge of its duties and functions, it is not amenable to the control of any other body", observed the Supreme Court. SC scrutinises executive and legislative decisions of the government to ensure that they do not breach the basic provisions of the Constitution. All explosive and divisive issues like caste, religion, region, language etc. that could have been the cause of conflict, have been judiciously resolved by the Supreme Court. CAG was entrusted with the crucial aspect of auditing the expenditure of central and state governments and check them from sliding into the jungle of corruption. SC has contempt of court power to punish those who attribute motives to its decisions and findings but CAG without any such power has often found itself caught in the crossfire between the ruling class and the opposition.

These and all other institutions have to stick to the constitutional tracks.

Responsibility for overlooking some of the pitfalls during the framing of the Constitution rests to some extent with framers and to a large extent with the subsequent short-sighted leaders due to their partisan vote-bank politics. One such pitfall was caste reservations. Castes have been the curse of India for centuries. To achieve their goal of 'divide-and-rule', reservation on caste basis was introduced by the British and subsequently it became impossible to eradicate these barriers. Debates in the Constituent Assembly recognised the bane of caste system and argued with vigour for introducing provisions in the Constitution to eradicate this social evil. Ambedkar, himself a victim of the caste system, said, "On 26th January, 1950, we are going to enter into a life of contradictions. In politics, we will have equality and in social and economic we will have inequality. If we continue to deny it for long, we will do so only by putting our political democracy in peril. We must remove this contradiction at the earliest possible moment or else those who suffer from inequality will blow up the structure of political democracy…" He also said "Political democracy cannot last unless there lies at the base of it social democracy." He was a crusader against untouchability and stood for the total annihilation of caste. Paradoxically, to eradicate caste system he inspired quotas for Scheduled Castes and Scheduled Tribes to make full citizens of those who had been banged down for centuries. These provisions perpetuated caste system rather than eradicate or minimise it. Ambedkar desired reservations to be just a tool to abolish the all-pervading caste system from public life. Reservation and its mechanics were not to be cast in stone and it was to be only a temporary device. Unfortunately, instead of achieving the goal of wiping out caste system from our social life, we have further widened its scope during the last 70 years. Short-term gains have resulted in long-term pain. History of caste reservations in India would have been different if our forefathers had displayed some grit and foresight in exploring some better alternatives. Advocates of caste-based reservation compromised the fundamental right of equality and laid more stress on social discrimination rather than on diminishing economic disparity. They were primarily responsible for laying boulders in the path of democracy which have further become stronger and the nation is paying heavily for this grave and destructive lapse.

From the very beginning, framers were apprehensive of the problems of democracy in India. In the last phases of the debate in the Constituent Assembly, Ambedkar said, "By independence, we have lost the excuse of blaming the British for anything going wrong. If thereafter things go wrong, we will have nobody to blame but ourselves." In his final address to the Constituent Assembly in November 1949, he said, "...there is a complete absence of two things in Indian society. One of them is equality. On the social plane, we have in India a society based on principles of graded inequality which means elevation of some and degradation of others. On the economic front, we have a society in which there are some who have immense wealth as against many that live in abject poverty…How long shall we continue to deny equality in our social and economic life?" At the conclusion of the Constituent Assembly, Rajendra Prasad, India's first President remarked, "To all we give the assurance that it will be our endeavour to end poverty and squalor and its companions-hunger and disease; to abolish distinction and exploitation and to ensure decent conditions for living." We were a nascent democracy with inevitable teething problems and all these noble thoughts reflected in these speeches on social and economic planes are sadly awaiting implementation. Ideas are the genesis of actions but they alone do not guarantee prosperity unless translated into action and judiciously implemented.

The best time for the implementation of some of the beneficial social and economic policies was at the time of promulgation of the Constitution. For equality it is paramount that all laws be uniformly applied to all citizens irrespective of any difference of caste, creed or religion. Unfortunately, the framers completely neglected this fundamental issue for petty political reasons and made the path of democracy most uneven and risky right from the very beginning. India is full of diversities and for equality Uniform Civil Code should have been an integral part of the Constitution. It was debated but sadly ignored and pushed to Directive Principles. Destination that was at arm's length then has now gone miles away.

On the whole only political considerations were kept in mind and social and economic issues were put on the back burner and no efforts were made during the framing of the Constitution or even afterwards towards these significant aspects. With all their wisdom, the framers pushed some of the noble thoughts under the carpet for succeeding generations. To implement these reforms became more and more difficult with the passage of time due to sectarian politics and conflicting interests of the various social groups. Opportunities, even with massive majority in Parliament, were squandered due to lack of political will, policy of appeasement and cheap vote-bank politics of narrow-minded politicians.

Before independence contention of many scholars, like John Stuart Mill, was that democracy is next to impossible in linguistically divided countries and that it will not survive in India. Similarly, Robert Dahl believed that widespread poverty and illiteracy are anathema to stable democracy. All these pessimists usually viewed India through the prism of caste, religion and region. Framers of the Constitution were well-aware of these problems and of vast diversities like religions, castes, creeds, faiths, beliefs, languages and numerous other factors as the stumbling blocks in the achievement of the cherished objectives of democracy. The creative thinkers were apprehensive that the path of Indian democracy is not going to be smooth. In fact, with the passage of time it has developed deeper and more dangerous pitfalls. Their fears and concerns are proving to be true. They will be trembling in their grave about the dangerous developments of democracy.

Foundation of an uneven path of Indian democracy was laid on the very day of its inception. Existing vast diversities continued to increase leading to undue social, economic and petty regional demands endangering the very existence of a stable democracy with its cherished ideals. Diversities are the stumbling blocks and a visible absence of sense of nationhood has constantly created problems in the successful implementation of the desired noble principles. Obstructionism by opportunistic leaders has gravely made the path laid with loose gravel even more uneven giving scope to the fears expressed by some in the beginning. It is now for the future generations to ensure the solemn implementation of the lofty objectives envisaged by the visionary framers. A good constitution could turn bad and a bad constitution could turn good, depending on the character and morality of people entrusted with its implementation. Ambedkar aptly remarked, "If things go wrong under the new Constitution, the reason will not be that we had a bad Constitution. What we will have to say is that Man was vile."

2

ON ROAD TO SOCIALISM

After independence Pandit Jawaharlal Nehru and Sardar Vallabh Bhai Patel, both Congressmen, were the two leaders who could lay their claim to be Prime Minister of India. Mahatma Gandhi who exercised great influence on Indian politics loved Nehru and decided in his favour. Patel had no option but to relent. In an appreciation of Nehru, he said, "We have worked together as lifelong friends and colleagues…valuing each other's advice…" Inwardly both had huge personality differences and were cut from different cloth. Both did not see eye to eye on many important issues but in national interest both remained "friends and colleagues." Their differences did not affect their loyalty to the nation unlike politicians of today who sacrifice national interests for their selfish political ends.

In the choice of Nehru as prime minister in preference to Patel, Gandhi unfairly overlooked Patel's claim and followed his emotions and personal liking for Nehru. He failed to realise that in those primitive years of independence India certainly needed a strong prime minister to take hard decisions and a statesman like Patel to hold reins of the country. It is likely that had Gandhi gone along with most of the Congress party and chosen Sardar Patel to be India's first prime minister, the course of history would have been quite different. It proved to be a grave political blunder and lack of far-sightedness of Gandhi as a statesman. Sarojini Naidu also favoured Patel and called him a veteran administrator and "man of decision and man of action."

Patel, hailed as India's Bismarck and 'Iron Man of India', was a seasoned statesman. He questioned Nehru's policy of meek submission to China on Tibet. A decade later, India's humiliation at the hands of China in 1962 led to the feeling that if Patel had lived long enough, he would have restrained Nehru. History of Kashmir would have also been different had Nehru acted on the sane advice of Patel for military action.

At the time of independence, India had 550 princely states. Integration of these states into Indian Union was a herculean task. Using a combination of negotiations, coercion and force was a master stroke of diplomacy and one of Patel's greatest contributions. Nehru would have never had the courage to take such bold steps and many Kashmirs would have been created inside India.

Besides political differences, Patel differed from Nehru on economic policy also. He believed in private enterprise and was not in favour of public sector. His views about business are more modern and if adopted then would have changed the course of India's economy. Apart from economic and political issues both differed on the point of secularism also. While Patel was fully committed to secularism and staunchly opposed communalism, Nehruvian secularism was an unfair appeasement of the minorities, a policy still followed by Congress. Nehru's ego and stubbornness laid the foundation of many knotty problems on account of which the nation is suffering even today.

To honour Patel's contribution to unify India, "Statue of Unity – *Ek Bharat, Shreshth Bharat*", was built in 2018 in Narmada district of Gujarat. The statue, tallest at 182 meters, is "nation's pride and world's marvel", and imbibes the concept of one nation, one people, and one culture.

In modern times two systems of formal economy belonging to somewhat opposing schools of thought are followed in the world. While in capitalism means of production, such as money and other forms of capital, are owned by private individuals, in socialism they are owned by the state. Under capitalism one works for one's own wealth but in socialism one works for wealth that in turn is distributed to everyone. Socialism essentially believes that the fruits of economic development reach the poor and marginalised to ensure equality. On the other hand, the serious drawback of capitalism is that it expands inequality and increases social tension. Comparing the two systems, Churchill remarked, "The inherent virtue of socialism is the equal sharing of miseries" and "The inherent vice of capitalism is the unequal sharing of blessings."

After independence Nehru did not consider capitalism or economic liberalisation as a viable option. His leaning towards socialism proved to be a great mistake in economic development of the country. Later global economic developments and disintegration of USSR are ample testimony to the failure of Nehru as a far-sighted economist.

With the passage of time India also endorsed the path of economic liberalisation. Capitalism was no longer considered 'sinful' to make money, so long as it was earned following taxation laws. Globally, capitalism is linked to greed and corruption and in India also liberal economy gave rise to a tide of scams and Congress became an active partner in its propagation.

On international diplomacy, Nehru's policy on Kashmir and China proved to be glaring examples of stark failure. The thorny problem of Kashmir still remains unsolved mainly due to his short-sightedness and India may pay for the lapse for years to come.

Same is the case with policy towards China. India's border dispute with China is a legacy of the British. Frontier between Tibet and Assam was negotiated by the British and McMahon Line was born on March 24, 1914. China refused to recognise McMahon Line and seized Tibet in mid-1930s. The Sino-Indian border today is the notional Line of Actual Control (LAC) which is not demarcated on any map.

The government of Peoples Republic of China (PRC) insisted the border to be re-negotiated but Nehru refused using legitimacy of the McMahon Line. *Panchsheel* Agreement and *'Hindi-Cheeny, bhai-bhai'* relationship forced him to recognise Tibet as a regime of China in 1954. Relations between the two countries deteriorated in 1959 due to Nehru's decision to give shelter to Dalai Lama, intern Tibetan migrants in India, and host Tibetan Government-in-exile. Calling Nehru a "stooge" and "running dog" of British and American imperialists, China wanted to give India a heavy punch.

It was against this surcharged backdrop that Nehru came up with 'Forward Policy' directing Indian troops to establish posts "as far forward as possible" from the then existing positions. Order to "throw the Chinese out" was given on September 22, 1962 and Nehru announced on October 11 that the army had been ordered to "free our territory".

The one-month long war between India and China was not a full-blown war and diplomatic relation was also not snapped. Explaining Chinese motive, British reporter James Cameron said, "This operation is to drive India, morally and economically, to the wall."

In the aftermath of the conflict, Lt. General TB Henderson Brooks and Brigadier Prem S Bhagat were asked to conduct "an operational review" of the Army's reverses. Parts of this 162-page top-secret classified report submitted in April 1963, only two original copies of which are known to exist, were revealed in March 2014. Keeping information secret beyond a reasonable period of time is inimical to an open democratic society. It prevents learning from past, and also impedes historical research and evolution of strategic thinking.

The report pointed out intelligence deficiencies, lack of coordination among intelligence agencies and shaky credibility of sources as the key problems that led to the debacle. Soldiers, equipped with canvas shoes and .303s were sent to snow-clad Himalayas. According to the report, the self-caused humiliating military collapse was due to Nehru's ill-timed 'Forward Policy' that "precipitated matters". Nehru was a very poor military strategist and, stubborn as he was, did not heed to take advice from the generals. War is a failure of diplomacy and this conflict was also a testimony to Nehru's diplomatic failure to settle the border dispute.

After 1962, China-India relations moved towards hostility and confrontation. Relations had ups and downs. Diplomatic and psychological warfare continues and the ghost of 1962 haunts and remains a lingering humiliation even today. A lesson of the Nehruvian blunder is that India must never let down its guard. Simultaneously, moving away from the shadow of history, try to achieve reasonable and just settlement of the territory in dispute in the larger interest of both the giant neighbouring powers.

The challenge before the leadership is to be pragmatic and harmonise reality with national aspirations to lead to lasting good relations with hostile neighbours for the growth of Indian democracy.

Nehru was a towering Indian personality but hesitated to take bold decisions in the interest of the nation. US President JF Kennedy, offered to help India detonate a nuclear device much before China did in 1964 but Nehru refused the offer. He never realised the need of making India militarily a strong nation. History would have been different if the offer had been accepted. US also offered India permanent membership of the UN Security Council virtually on a platter but Nehru declined in favour of China. India lost an important place in global power due to the short-sighted generosity of Nehru. Boundary dispute with China would have also been settled amicably if Nehru had accepted an oblique proposal of China of east-west swap and conceded uninhibited Aksai Chin where, as he said, "not a blade of grass grows.

Nehru's notion of non-alignment prevented India from becoming a tool in the hands of either of the two super powers thus disallowing them to use our territory for their own political and strategic advantage. The policy, though mocked at by many then and even now is praiseworthy. It gave India a voice in the world and was in conformity with our policy of peace and non-violence.

He also played a critical role in supporting anti-colonial and decolonisation movements throughout the world.

Nehru is a subject of sharp criticism today due to his political, social and economic failings. His policy of centralised state planning kept India back for decades. His policy on social reforms, particularly exceedingly slow advancement in improving literacy, is a stark example of misplaced priorities. His repeated statements on Kashmir saying that he did not know 'what to do', mistaken 'forward policy' on China ignoring the warning of the Generals and inability to take a decision on UCC are all testimony to the fact that Nehru was a confused statesman. His diplomatic failings on Kashmir and naïve trust in the Chinese, embodied in the slogan, *'Hindi-Cheeny, bhai-bhai'* are, very appalling. With Patel gone there was none to check his dictatorial and highly confused exercise of authority. It is also believed that during the initial period of independence Nehru's policies were influenced to a large extent by Lord Mountbatten due to Nehru's intimate personal relations with his wife, Edwina Mountbatten. Contents of lot of files on the subject and letters exchanged between them have not been made public by UK government as they would affect bilateral relations between India and Great Britain. Once these files are made public history of the influence of these personal relations and their impact on Indian policies during the initial years of independence may be rewritten.

Nehru's policy of socialism may not be doubted in accordance with time for socialism was considered relevant for a country like India where economic inequality was pervasive and fighting poverty and hunger, the greatest enemies of humanity, was the first priority. His successors hesitated to change with the vast global changes and blindly continued the faulty economic and development policies. They did not follow liberalisation, establishment of industries and foreign investment but strengthened 'inspector *raj*' and nationalisation. Asian countries with close relationship to the US opened up their economies in the 1970s, resulting in their economic boom. India missed the opportunity and gave China a chance to become a super power. India suffered due to these hesitations and continues to suffer.

Nehru's defenders defend him as a crusader of democracy. Man is to be judged on parameters he was best placed in. With the wisdom and experience of today we can say that democratic institutions at that initial stage of their inception could have been deeply strengthened if Nehru had been little more far-sighted. Opportunity to enforce UCC was sadly missed which still remains a grave social casualty. Education and health were completely neglected and no effort was made even in coming decades also by our lukewarm leaders towards eradication of poverty. China gained independence almost simultaneously with India and was a victim of similar problems. Though the systems of government were different, China made tremendous progress towards literacy, economic development and in minimising caste differences. Nehru dominated the polity after independence and was in a much stronger position to introduce vast social, political and economic reforms but was a reluctant reformer.

Nehru was not an admirer of ancient Indian culture and considered ancient history to be 'deadwood of the past'. He was more obsessed with western culture and, divorced from the poor, he could never realise pangs of poverty and his economic policies did not try to eradicate this worst social malice. By faith, Nehru was also not a great believer in religions. He wrongfully associated Hinduism, with prejudice, superstition and mechanical ritual. His views on religion differed from those of Gandhi who, even as a Hindu, was devoutly pious to all religions. Both, however, considered that all religions in India should be respected and the state should be above religious bias. In 1948, in one of his first letters to chief ministers, Nehru wrote, "We have a Muslim minority who are so large in numbers that they cannot, even if they want to go anywhere else. They have got to live in India." He also said, co-existence in India is not an option but a compulsion. Some of Nehru's policies and those of some successors have given an idea of appeasement of minorities. It was mainly due to vote-bank politics rather than any good-will gesture to the minorities.

For the last seven decades Nehru-Gandhi dynasty has been perpetuated and this has become a cause of Nehru's criticism. In face of stiff opposition from his senior colleagues, he got Indira Gandhi elected as Congress President in 1959 that paved way for her to be prime minister as per tradition in the Congress party. Active dynastic feudalism by his successors certainly closed doors for many aspiring and intelligent Congressmen to break the dynastic citadel which was soon bereft of good leadership. There was no dearth of capable leaders from outside the dynasty but dynastic greed, particularly after Rajiv Gandhi, did not allow anyone to come up. Paradoxically, Congress adopted democracy for the country but is most undemocratic in its own home that has led to its downfall.

Though Nehru did not directly try to promote dynastic rule, he certainly did not tolerate any ones' dominance. Sardar Patel and Dr. Shyama Prasad Mookerjee are significant examples. Mookerjee was a member of the Nehru cabinet which he quit over Article 370 and died under mysterious circumstances in a Kashmir jail while leading an agitation against this constitutional provision. Nehru nurtured diversity in his government as his team of 14 members of Cabinet had five non-Congressmen. Some critics, however, believe that this was more due to his authoritarian nature to keep experienced Congressmen out of the government rather than any sense of generosity to nurture diversity.

History gives people the privilege of hindsight which can be over-generous or unfairly dismissive. Nehru had his failures but his singularity in strengthening foundations of our young Republic in its formative years through his passionate commitment to democracy, thereby ensuring political stability of the country, cannot be minimised. He faced huge challenge to build a prosperous India out of the "mud and filth" left behind by colonialism, as Tagore said. With all the criticism, Nehru is responsible for institutionalising democracy in India when he could easily have been a dictator. With India's size and diversity, democracy is the only guarantee for its stability as its failure is an invitation to disintegration. Nehru's failures are many but this singular achievement is significant.

Democracy that Nehru nurtured was vibrant in spirit but crippled in reality. Political institutions were somewhat strengthened but socially and economically the country was completely ignored. The damsel of democracy survived during first two decades after independence but the path generally remained rough and patchy. Road to social developments was full of pebbles and thorns, and made economic policies lope-sided which could not be stabilised for over four decades. The path of Indian democracy remained uneven and continued to suffer with the passage of time.

3

THE DANGEROUS BEND

Heart-broken by defeat at the hands of China and apparent failure of his much cherished *Panchsheel* policy, Nehru died on 27 May, 1964. He had never tried to groom any successor and prospects of doom were feared. Active dynastic feudalism did not prevail at that time and a member of Nehru-Gandhi family was not considered a successor. Lal Bahadur Shastri was unanimously elected as Nehru's successor and he became Prime Minister of India on June 2, 1964. Democracy survived and succeeded in the test of succession.

Shastri was shy and soft-spoken by nature who maintained a low profile in public life. He was non-threatening, modest, unassuming homegrown person completely opposite of Nehru and "had hardly made any enemy in his entire career." He was a family man who even "put out his bathing soap to dry in the sun after use to ensure it lasted longer." He was a pragmatic statesman, a true nationalist and service to the nation was his first priority. As railway minister earlier, he owned moral responsibility for a major train accident and resigned, thus setting a very high standard of morality, completely absent from the life of our present-day politicians devoid of ethical values. He was honest to the core, died as a poor person, and only owned a Fiat car bought on installments, whose loan had not been fully paid till his death. Overshadowed by the aura of Nehru, he had the challenge to fit in his big boots. Courage and boldness to take even difficult decisions in the interest of the nation was his paramount quality. In the context of Indo-Pak conflict, a General aptly remarked, "The Army could never forget the tallest order from the shortest man." He proved that courage is not in six feet of length but in six inches of head.

Due to some grave blunders of Nehru, Shastri inherited a shattered economy with high inflation and terrible scarcity of food. Confidence-level of the forces was also low on account of the devastating defeat at the hands of the Chinese.

Nehru did not focus on agriculture and food problem was very grim. America decided to pay a loan of USD 600 million a year to India for the solution of agriculture problem. It also passed a law, called PL-80, and allowed sale of wheat to developing countries in their local currencies. This was suspected to be a sinister ploy to keep the developing countries like India poor and underdeveloped. India imported fourteen million MT of food grain, the cost being more than one-and-a-half billion USD.

To solve the acute food problem, Shastri gave top priority to agricultural reforms. C Subramaniam, minister of food and agriculture in his Cabinet, was a dynamic, bold and intelligent minister. To provide more incentive to the farmers he raised the price of wheat by 15% in the face of stiff opposition. Indian democracy is not used to taking bold political decisions and Subramaniam was criticised by Cabinet, Congress party and the powerful Left for a "sellout to America" but the prime minister and the intellectual elite supported his dynamism. He announced his new agriculture policy and arranged import of 16,000 MT of high-yield wheat miracle seed that transformed the harvests. The "Green Revolution" made India self-sufficient in food and the boom placed Indian agriculture on a growth path. Wheat production rose by 5.5% per annum for the next decade from less than 1% between 1905 and 1945 and 3% during 1950-51.

Shastri was a far-sighted statesman, a man of determination and action but unfortunately life and time were not on his side. He could not further develop and strengthen his policies of economic liberalisation due to a futile and bloody war thrust upon India by Pakistan. The founder of *'Jai Jawan, Jai Kissan'* slogan, which echoes even today through the length and breadth of the country, inflicted a crushing defeat on the forces of Pakistan that brought the enemy to her knees. Soviet Union wanted both countries to arrive at a mutually acceptable agreement and prime ministers of India and

Pakistan met at the fabled city of Tashkent. While the country was still rejoicing the triumph of Shastri, news of his death on 11 January 1966 completely shattered the nation. He died of heart attack under mysterious circumstances within hours of signing the peace treaty. His death has remained a complete mystery till today and circumstances leading to his death have never been properly investigated by any government. By signing the treaty Shastri shed his personal ego and displayed great qualities of statesmanship. For valour and admirable skill of the forces, Indian nation shall always remain indebted to him. He was one of those Indians who left an indelible imprint on the people and the forces. He shared the ideals, hopes and aspirations of common man and imbibed, cherished and respected democratic values in his personal and political life. His life was perhaps the greatest loss to the nation that could have duly compensated for the deficiencies of Nehru and the miscalculated adventures of Indira.

Nehru's death did not end an era, Shastri's did. With no provision for a successor, Congress party was once again thrown in a maze of confusion. During Nehru's last days, some of the powerful central and state leaders under Congress President K Kamraj had formed an informal group, known as 'Syndicate', for directing the Congress policies in the post-Nehru era. In a masterstroke of diplomacy, the brilliant strategist allowed Congress Parliamentary Party to choose their leader by secret ballot in order to defeat Morarji Desai, a conservative and very rigid authoritarian. Magic of Indira Gandhi's most respected surname and belief of the Syndicate that she would be a '*maum ki gudia*' (doll of wax) or '*goongi-gudia*' (dumb doll) worked in her favour and in a bitter contest she defeated Morarji. The belief of the Congress party bosses and Syndicate that she will dance to their tunes like a puppet and would be a "malleable and disposable figurehead" proved to be a grave miscalculation and the '*goongi-gudia*' turned out to be one of the most controversial prime ministers of India. Born lucky, luck was thrust upon her and inexperienced Indira Gandhi became India's first woman prime minister on 24 June 1966 at the age of 48.

Indira Priyadarshini was born in a highly aristocratic family on November 19, 1917 and was the only child of Jawaharlal and Kamla Nehru. Her mother died when she was y0ung and she was always surrounded by a pack of servants, English nannies, two tough sisters of Nehru and a dominant and extremely dynamic father. Deprived of parental care, she constantly craved for love and affection. Loneliness, anxiety, and a feeling of insecurity in early childhood, made her more introverted and withdrawn. Childhood problems were further compounded with an unhappy marriage to Feroz Gandhi who died in 1960. All these problems of personal life had a devastating impact on her personality. To a large extent they were responsible for her authoritarian and arrogant behaviour, a feeling of distrust for the people and taking controversial decisions in political career.

Politics was in the blood of Indira Gandhi and her complete upbringing was amidst political upheavals of India. She had served as member of various committees of Congress, had been President All-India Congress Committee and Minister for Information and Broadcasting in Shastri's Cabinet. With all this vast political experience she had still no reputation as an able administrator. She had no clear notion of political theory and frankly admitted, "I don't really have a political philosophy."

On becoming Prime Minister, Indira Gandhi inherited a host of economic and political problems and faced many challenges. Foreign exchange was at its rock bottom, Five-year Plans had gone awry and industrial production was at its low ebb. To add to all these, corruption was rampant and under-currents of political turmoil were evident due to disgruntled opposition within the party. In her compulsion and desperate need to seek political support from non-Congress parties, she agreed to the demand of Akali Dal for the creation of Punjabi Suba in 1966 and created Himachal Pradesh, Haryana and Punjab. She also conceded to the demand of Akalis for Chandigarh but it could not be implemented due to demand of two districts of Punjab by Haryana which was refused by Punjab. The settlement has still remained a dead letter and Chandigarh remains a Union Territory (UT). She also conceded to Naga rebels demand for autonomy to silence unrest in the far-east. Insecure from childhood and ambitious by nature, she systematically alienated and expelled leaders of standing and tried to remove all political adversaries that came her way. Groupism and factionalism became more predominant in the party and prestige of Parliament as a cardinal democratic institution also suffered. Opposition parties with divergent views and ideologies joined hands to form anti-Congress fronts and she became the target of attack both inside and outside the Parliament.

In a clash of violent egos and autocratic style of functioning, Indira Gandhi soon began to lose grip over the people and her own colleagues in the party. In the General Elections in 1967, Congress won but lost over a hundred seats and Syndicates were critical of the "dismal performance" under her leadership. Confrontation developed between her and Morarji Desai who was silenced by accommodating him as Deputy Prime Minister. Internal situation of the country also started deteriorating fast paving way for a dangerous experiment in the history of Indian democracy.

Relations between government and organisational wing of Congress had always been sour since the time of Nehru. The party wanted the government to consult it on all important matters. Nehru argued that responsibility for decision making must rest with the government and to hold the prime minister accountable to the party would reduce parliamentary democracy to a "mockery". With Indira Gandhi, the confrontation again cropped up. She declared that "…here is a question of whom the party wants and whom the people want. My position among the people is uncontested." She asserted that the prime minister had the unbridled will in the parliamentary form of democracy and this fundamental point became the main issue of all future clashes. Stubborn, as she was, her authoritarian attitude crushed democracy within the party. Her private secretaries, took independent ministerial decisions that further damaged the democratic system.

To strengthen her position, Indira Gandhi adopted a radical Ten-Point Programme which included social control over banks, nationalisation of general insurance, state trading in import and export, ceiling on urban property and income, and curb on business monopolies. Privy purse and other privileges of erstwhile Maharajas, guaranteed to them on joining the Indian union were abolished. The move, lost in Rajya Sabha, was enforced by a Presidential ordinance but struck down by the Supreme Court.

Suspicious and insecure by nature, and stifled by the "Old Guard", she took one of the greatest gambles of her political career and decided to engineer a vertical split in the Congress Parliamentary Party. The opportunity came in May 1969 with the sudden demise of President Zakir Husain. The Syndicates favoured Neelam Sanjiva Reddy. She openly supported VV Giri, Vice-president of India. In a master stroke of shrewd diplomacy like an astute politician, she came out with the idea of inner-party democracy, suggested "free vote" and diverted the attention from personal ambition of political power acquisition to ideological one. Giri won by a very narrow margin.

In a fit of revenge, Congress President Nijalingappa expelled Indira Gandhi and her henchmen from the party for violating party discipline and directed Congress Parliamentary Party to elect a new leader, leading to a split in the 84-year old Indian National Congress creating two working committees and two Congress Parliamentary Parties. The two groups were subsequently named Congress (O) – for 'Old' and Congress (I) for 'Indira'. The purge and defections reduced Indira Gandhi to minority in the Parliament but she managed to continue with the outside support of communists, DMK, Akalis and BKD. She faced ten no-confidence motions ever since she became prime minister.

With all attention on destroying the opponents, reforms and democracy were the worst sufferers. Shashi Tharoor has rightly observed, "As the magnetic pull of nationalism faded, loyalty to the Congress as an institution declined." In their ambition to grab and retain power, both factions of Congress began to turn to opposition. Political defections became astonishingly frequent. Moral or ideological values began to be shed conveniently and party affiliation now became a matter of convenience. Foundation of a new and dangerous path of factionalism and joining hands with parties of divergent ideologies began to be laid in democracy. Performance was sacrificed at the altar of power that gave birth later on to horse-trading which many subsequent governments followed with impunity and has continued till today.

Indira Gandhi reaped the success of agricultural reforms of Shastri and began to be hailed a deity by her sycophants. Her economic policies projected her as champion of economic reforms for the welfare of the people and as leader of the masses. She wanted to cash on her popularity. In a move of deft diplomacy, she announced general elections in 1971, a year before they were actually due. Her bitter opponents could not bear her growing popularity and raised the slogan of *'Indira hatao'*. To counter their attack, she gave the pro-poor slogan, *'garibi hatao'*, giving the masses a ray of hope for their prosperity. In the wave created by her charisma, she trounced the Grand Alliance of both Congress and non-Congress opponents and led her Congress to a resounding victory. Intoxicated by her powerful position, she crucified democracy and imposed state chief ministers of her choice, suspended intra-Congress elections and undermined judiciary. State governments were dismissed at will under Article 356. President's Rule that was used by the centre twenty times during the first two decades of independence, was invoked seventy times for next two decades from 1967.

Conflicts shifted from ideological to personal levels and any hostility to her party was interpreted as anti-national. Appointments began to be made on the basis of personal loyalties, ignoring merit. She pushed through series of amendments including one giving right to Parliament to alter the fundamental rights. Sacred public and democratic institutions like Parliament and bureaucracy that are supposed to nurture democracy were crushed under her authoritarian foot promoting corruption, nepotism, incompetence and criminality.

Opportunity to exercise her authority also came her way from the international field. In the general elections in 1970 in East Bengal, also called East Pakistan after India's partition, Sheikh Mujibur Rehman, leader of Awami League won one of the most impressive mandates and proclaimed independence of 'Bangladesh'. Indira Gandhi recognised the provisional government of Bangladesh and in December 1971, Indian army crossed the border to help *Mukti Bahini,* freedom fighters of Bangladesh. In a decisive war, Pakistani forces surrendered on 16 December. East Pakistan was liberated and Indira Gandhi became a hero among the Indian masses.

Intoxicated by her Bangladesh success, Indira Gandhi successfully tested the first nuclear device, 'Smiling Buddha', in 1974 in Pokhran desert in Rajasthan. Though Nehru followed non-proliferation, she refused to sign the nuclear ordinance and made it clear that like non-violence and non-alignment, non-proliferation was no longer Indian policy. Attention to internal social and economic developments at this stage would have made Indira

Gandhi one of the greatest prime ministers in the history of India. Shashi Tharoor very aptly remarked, "Mrs. Gandhi was skilled at the acquisition and maintenance of power, but hopeless at wielding of it forever." It is an irony of fate that the road of Indian democracy took a dangerous bend due to the authoritarian and insecure nature of Indira Gandhi.

Popularity of Indira Gandhi declined with the failure of social and economic developments, spurt in prices of oil, rampant inflation, food riots, railway strike, decrease in industrial production, unemployment, corruption, and mutiny of Armed Constabulary in UP. Agitations in Bihar and Gujarat turned the socio-economic discontent into a political movement. Wide spread agitations, '*gheraos*' and '*bandhs*' became order of the day. "Total Revolution" led by her strong political opponent, Jayaprakash Narayan, more popularly known as JP or '*Lok Nayak*' completely paralised the administration. He wrote to her, "… please do not identify yourself with the nation. You are not immortal, India is." Massive student movement in Gujarat which soon spread to Bihar and other parts of the country further added to her woes. She stream-rolled her opponents whom she dubbed as politically corrupt persons of dubious patriotic convictions. Cabinet Minister CD Deshmukh remarked that India suffered "…economic and sociological handicaps in the establishment of democracy."

Unfortunately for Indira Gandhi, all these serious political and social problems coincided with a crushing blow to her political career. Raj Narain, her resolute opponent in her own Rai Bareli constituency, filed a case in the court for misuse of official machinery by her during electioneering in 1971. After four years, on 12 June 1975, Justice Jagmohanlal Sinha of Allahabad High Court found her guilty on the technicality of electoral malpractices. Her election win from Rae Bareli was declared null and void and she was banned for contesting elections for another six years. This was like "firing the Prime Minister for a traffic ticket." She filed an appeal before the Supreme Court.

Apprehending an adverse decision by the Apex Court and fearing political isolation, Indira Gandhi decided to strike back immediately. On June 25, 1975, she wrote to President, Fakhruddin Ali Ahmed, with a copy of the draft for the proclamation of Emergency, "…information has reached us which indicates that there is an imminent danger to the security of India being threatened by internal disturbances." The draft was taken to the President for his signatures before midnight without putting the information before the Cabinet and was justified on the ground of extreme urgency. The President immediately signed and issued "Proclamation of Emergency" under powers conferred on him under clause (1) of Article 352 of the Constitution. President's meek capitulation and the abject surrender of the Cabinet and other ministers gave a crushing blow to the "secular democratic republic" damaging the basic fabric of Indian democracy for a few years.

Leaders of the Grand Alliance, including Jayaprakash Narayan, were arrested for spreading "sedition" and sent to unknown destinations. Press and electronic media became the first victims of Emergency and complete censorship was imposed on them. Deputy Minister for Information and Broadcasting, Dharam Bir Sinha, justified by saying, "What we, therefore, need in Indian journalism today is a spirit of inquiry rather than the luxury of opinions."

The committed judiciary in a majority of four-to-one succumbed to the government pressure. Civil liberties were suspended and fundamental rights including habeas-corpus was curtailed thereby suspending the democratic rights of the people. Justice HR Khanna penned a loud, lone dissent and reiterated that fundamental right to life could never be suspended. He was superseded and Beg became CJI. He resigned. In his autobiography, 'Neither Roses Nor Thorns', he said "There arose a feeling of some satisfaction for having not swerved or faltered at the crucial time from what I believe was the correct course." His full-size portrait hangs in Court No. 2 in SC to remind all SC judges about his singular contribution to keep judiciary intact by insulating it from politicians.

In clause 49 of Forty-second Amendment to the Constitution, unrestrained opposition, free and critical press and independence of judiciary were all severely curtailed. Prime Minister was taken out of the gambit of election disputes. Indira Gandhi consistently bypassed the Parliament and Cabinet and crushed the federal initiatives.

'Power corrupts and absolute power corrupts absolutely.' Sanjay Gandhi, Indira Gandhi's elder son, became the "Extra Constitutional Centre of Power" and subverted almost every democratic institution. Sycophancy became the order of the day. It is said that once Sanjay Gandhi's slipper fell, and in a race to please him, three chief ministers ran to pick it up. He introduced his own "five-point programme" of population control, slum clearance, tree-planting, literacy improvement and dowry abolition. Though the agenda was laudable, it miserably failed on all fronts. BK Nehru, Indira Gandhi's cousin said that Sanjay Gandhi "destroyed all the fragile democratic institutions." Supporting her son, Indira Gandhi said, "he made the trains run on time".

Imposition of Emergency had some immediate favourable reaction. Visibly, public life began to improve. Bribes and frustration of standing in long queues for petty domestic needs and services virtually came to an end. Schools, colleges, universities and other public institutions, regularly paralised by rioting and unions, reopened. Strikes and lockouts in factories completely vanished. Labour in factories became more productive and production rose by 10.5%. Loss of man-days dropped by 74% and power supply rose by 13%. Demonstrations, disturbances and absenteeism or late arrival in offices was almost negligible. Services like train and plane became normal and punctual. Black marketers, unscrupulous hoarders, hijackers of public transport and smugglers were put behind bar. Supply of food stuff became more regular and prices of essential commodities came down bringing much-needed relief to the poor and middle class. Undeclared capital virtually dried up thus strengthening the health of economy. There was also greater thrust for constitutional changes to facilitate the attainment of socio-economic progress. At this time, per capita income was approximately $ 100 per year and Newsweek wrote, "In India, it is more important to be fed than to be free."

Emergency indirectly confirmed the fact that we had not yet learnt to respect law and were disciplined only under the rule of rod. Vinoba Bhave called the new order '*Anushasan Parva*', a period of discipline. Indira Gandhi also described Emergency as "Disciplined Democracy" and was congratulated by some but condemned by most.

Indira Gandhi had feared a "plot" against the state though there was no evidence to justify any "grand design" to overthrow her government. She defended Emergency by saying that choice was between democracy for few and social justice for the down-trodden many. According to her, unbridled democratic freedom and existence of flourishing democracy had resulted in organised opportunism and thwarted social and economic progress of the country. In a nationwide broadcast she said that excesses of Indian democracy weakened the capacity of the national government to act decisively towards economic development. Her Law Minister, HR Gokhale's justification was that, "if the power is required by the authority for the good of the people, the possibility of abuse should not be used as an argument for denying such power to the authority concerned." Worshipers of Gandhian principles argued that end must justify means and did not support Emergency as means for any good of the people. They believed that democracy had been crucified.

Indira Gandhi proclaimed a "twenty-point programme" for raising the standard of common man which included rural improvement schemes, mass education and abolition of bonded labour. Unfortunately, all these noble ideas were only confined to official files and she miserably failed to improve social or economic condition of the masses. "India is Indira and Indira is India" remained only a hollow slogan.

Arguments in favour or against the gains of Emergency are very complex. History does not provide any proof that suspension of democracy can deliver political, social or economic efficiency. Authority alone does not justify efficiency as tyranny completely destroys democratic institutions. There was widespread criticism in the West on the imposition of Emergency. It was believed that the experiment of democracy in a pluralist country had come to a sad end.

Mercifully the dark chapter in the history of Indian democracy soon came to an end and no serious damage was done to the Republic of India. Emergency effectively lasted 19 months and India escaped the possibility of slipping into an authoritarian rule. A note dated March 21, 1977 that remained buried for 30 years reads, "Cabinet has decided to recommend to the President to revoke the proclamation of Emergency…" Almost immediately several draconian laws like curb on freedom of expression were withdrawn and the country limped to normalcy.

Intoxicated by her false achievements, Indira Gandhi remained in complete darkness of the erosion of her popularity. Her sycophants assured her that if Emergency was lifted she would win the elections by a thumping majority. Convinced of her success, she announced general election. Main opposition parties, except Communist Party, merged to form Janta Party and even the loyalists deserted her. Indira Gandhi lost her own parliamentary seat to Raj Narain and fell from the pinnacle of power to the electoral dustbin of defeated stalwarts. Sanjay Gandhi was also defeated. This was a testimony to the strength of democracy in India.

Reins of the government now fell into the hands of Janta Party. After much wrangling, Morarji Desai became Prime Minister and the first non-Congress government came to power on March 24, 1977. Political coalition of Janta government soon disintegrated due to in-fighting.

Instead of devoting their time to good governance and winning over the goodwill of the people, they made the suicidal mistake of prosecuting Indira Gandhi and her son. Such vindictive actions of the government proved to be futile and Indira Gandhi gained sympathy of the people which paved way for her comeback. She was elected to Lok Sabha in a by-election from Chikmagalur in Karnataka in August 1978 but her election was declared void and she was expelled from the House in January 1979.

Janta Party proved to be an unstable coalition and the inglorious rule of heterogeneous forces based on personal ambitions and opportunistic politics came to an end. Morarji Desai, a very stubborn character and not deft to handle the divergent political forces, was replaced by Charan Singh but he was also forced to quit after six months. Parliament was dissolved and fresh elections were called by the end of 1979.

There was no suitable alternative with the electorate and Congress was once again voted to power in January 1980. This election for the first time witnessed more incidents of booth-capturing, musclemen threatening or bribing the officials to allow them to stamp ballot-papers with their candidate's name and use of weapons to threaten the voters. All these were signs of the beginning of criminalisation of politics which became more prominent with the passage of time. Sanjay Gandhi also won the Lok Sabha seat from Amethi, Uttar Pradesh but while recklessly flying a stunt plane in defiance of local regulations, he was killed in an air crash on 23 January 1980. Sarcastically, it is said that if he had lived he would have done to the country what he did to the plane.

Indira Gandhi was impulsive by nature and performed two dangerous experiments with Indian democracy. In one she tarnished democracy and brought disgrace to her own image and in the other she tried to save democracy from disintegration and lost her life. In 1974 Akali Dal in Punjab adopted Anandpur Sahib Resolution ostensibly demanding for all states the autonomy guaranteed to them under the Constitution. Indira Gandhi lacked the diplomatic fore-sight and ability to deal with such situations. To counterfeit their activities, she encouraged and reportedly even financed Sant Jarnail Singh Bhindrawale, a fundamentalist and young religious preacher. 'Fire is a good servant but a bad master' and it became essential for Indira Gandhi to destroy the monster created and nourished by her. As a shrewd man, Bhindrawale betrayed Indira Gandhi, joined the Akalis and took up the cause of an independent state. Golden Temple, one of the most sacred shrines of the Sikhs which symbolises the spiritual authority of God, was turned into an armed citadel and '*Akal Takth*', symbol of His temporal authority, into a refuge of terrorists. It is believed that arms were smuggled in trucks bringing ration for the *gurudwara* kitchen.

Suspicious of sinister activities of the treacherous combination of Akalis and Jarnail Singh clique, Indira

Gandhi imposed President's rule in Punjab in late 1983. Bhindrawale moved into the precincts of Golden Temple which was surrounded by army. '*Akal Takth*' was wrecked by tanks in 'Operation Blue Star' and forces of Jarnail Singh were flushed with his death. Some of Indira Gandhi's bitter critics believe that instead of dispatching armed forces, she could have starved the holders into submission. Her major political miscalculation was riding the lion which she could not control.

'Operation Blue Star' deeply hurt sentiments of the Sikhs. Sikh extremists swore blood for blood to avenge the attack on their sacred shrine. Indira Gandhi and many army generals involved in the attack were on their hit list. General AS Vaidya, the then Army Chief, was shot dead in Pune's cantonment area. Eight assassination attempts have so far been made on the life of 87-year old Lt. Gen. Kuldeep Singh Brar for leading the commando force.

Indira Gandhi paid price with her life and was assassinated by the forces of extremism that she herself had primed for narrow partisan purposes. Two of her bodyguards, Beant Singh and Satwant Singh, pumped pistol and Sten gun bullets into her frail body on the morning of 31ˢᵗ October 1984 and silenced forever the voice of the 'Iron Lady of India'. Beant Singh was shot dead while Satwant Singh and another conspirator, Kehar Singh, were hanged on January 6, 1989. In her last speech Indira Gandhi said, as if making a prophecy, "I do not worry whether I live or not. As long as there is any breath in me, I will go on serving you. When I die, every single drop of my blood will give strength to India and sustain united India."

Indira Gandhi's assassination shook the nation. Retaliation engineered by political leaders with the active assistance of law enforcement agencies followed in Delhi and other parts of the country. Five to ten thousand innocents lost their lives and property worth crores was destroyed. For decades the victims have waited in vain for justice but none has been punished for this brazen mayhem. The involvement of some senior Congress ministers and leaders, like HKL Bhagat (died in 2005), Sajjan Kumar and Jagdish Tytler was credibly alleged. Some infer moral, political and even legal culpability of the highest levels, including Rajiv Gandhi who did not want the massacre investigated. Recommendations of commissions and committees were either ineffective or were brazenly cast aside. Court cases against the instigators and some Congress politicians were filed in the courts and decisions are ironically still pending. Sajjan Kumar was finally implicated, and sentenced on December 17, 2018 by Delhi high court "for the remainder of his life". The riots were termed "genocide" and "carnage against humanity" and Delhi police was censured for "abject failure" in probing the violence. Such sickening episodes tarnish the secular character of our democracy.

Those who cannot learn from history are condemned to repeat it. What India needs is reforms that will make ministers and police officers legally liable for such mass crimes. The government in power cannot escape the responsibility for such wanton acts which they fail to prevent despite being in a position to do so. Rahul Gandhi, once President of the Congress party, acknowledged in an interview in February, 2014, that workers of the then ruling Congress may have been involved in the Delhi carnage. But this was more a political eyewash than a sincere apology of the carnage.

Sixteen years of political dominance of Indira Gandhi, one of the most powerful women of Indian democracy and the most controversial of the Nehru-Gandhi dynasty, came to a tragic end. She created the same upheavals in the working of democracy in India as the steep ups and downs of her personal life. The experiment of Emergency was "most damaging moment in India's timeline" and one of the most dangerous experiments which fortunately did not destroy the sacred fabric of Indian Republic. The modern American theologian Niebuhr rightly remarked, "The perils of uncontrolled power are perennial reminders of virtues of a democratic society."

Majority of people criticise Indira Gandhi for her destruction of the sacred institution of democracy and are of the opinion that Emergency was not necessary and was proclaimed solely and purely for political purposes. The nefarious method adopted by her was not necessary and certainly avoidable. Unfortunately, she tried to kill a fly with a gun. President Pranab Mukerjee in his book 'The Dramatic Decade: the Indira Gandhi Years' says that the Emergency was perhaps an "avoidable event" and Congress and Indira Gandhi had to pay a heavy price for this "misadventure". He also wrote, "…many of us who were part of the Union Cabinet at that time…did not then understand its deep and far reaching impact." She miserably failed to understand the nature of vast, varied and defused Indian society and did not realise that in a country with multiple diversities, it is impossible to sustain over-centralisation.

Indira Gandhi wrecked critical democratic institutions. Constitution amendments enforced by her have been widely criticised by the intellectuals. All such amendments were subsequently repealed by the succeeding Janta Government. Curbing powers of judiciary, the strongest pillar of our democratic system and a more effective agent of change than even the Parliament, was unwarranted. She had once remarked, "The purpose of democracy is to involve more and more people in policy-making." Ironically, she took a complete U-turn and had only a handful of sycophants as her advisors during Emergency. Her argument that democracy was impeding social justice also cannot hold ground. She enjoyed parliamentary majority but failed to bring about the desired reforms.

Indira Gandhi was a lion-hearted lady and this 'Iron Lady' is one of the most popular prime ministers the country has produced. Her failing was that instead of adopting alternative democratic methods of strengthening the existing system, she tried to weaken it by her dominance over judiciary, press, principle of collective cabinet responsibility and powers of the Parliament. She is also blamed to have injected venom of factionalism, criminalisation of politics, and authoritarian style in the political system.

Indira Gandhi's declaration of Emergency and later victory in elections has two vital lessons for Indian and world democracies. Firstly, even democracy is not perfect and uncontrolled power in it is a perennial reminder of the perils of democracy crawling into the hands of dictatorship. Secondly, even dictatorship can be defeated by democratic means to restore democracy. Victory of Janta government also confirmed the beauty of democracy that underdogs can also come on the top and the principle of survival of the strongest and fittest is by no means absolute in democracy.

The failure of Emergency demonstrated that proper mobilisation of people can change the course of democracy. To quote Niebuhr again, "Man's capacity for justice makes democracy possible; but man's inclination to injustice makes democracy necessary." Emergency, however, confirmed the weaknesses of democracy that fails to control corruption, criminalisation of politics, politicisation of criminality, and ability to take firm decisions in the larger interest of the nation. It also confirmed that a democracy that fails to make social and economic changes for the welfare of the people is bound to suffer at some point of time.

Emergency was not devoid of some significant lessons. It proved that, as a nation that had remained slave for centuries, we are more inclined to the rule of rod and less to a sense of self-discipline. Corruption and inefficiency have taken such a deep root in our lives that we are not prepared to shed it without use of strict rule of law and even brutal force. Dom Moraes defended the experiment of Indira Gandhi and said, "She is the only politician in India with a thoroughly modern mind… Without this ruthlessness, this autocratic touch, nothing would ever be done about anything in India." Majority of people also believe that freedom is less important than bread and only a very strong government can achieve socio-economic reforms.

The sharp and dangerous bend in the democratic system of India that Indira Gandhi tried to venture was soon straightened by her and the sacred institution of democracy survived from the onslaught of despots as it has survived everywhere. Its short period proved to be a blessing as its furtherance could have been disastrous to the largest democracy of the world and could have also adversely affected the life of democracies in other parts of the world.

To safeguard Indian democracy from a repeat of Emergency we need a vibrant judiciary, an unfettered media and a strong civil society. Ideology-less veneration of the powerful is the dangerous block that tempts the greedy politicians to sacrifice noble principles at the altar of selfishness, material rewards and furtherance of self-interest. As Tulsidas aptly puts it: *Sur nar muni sab ki yeha riti, swartha lagi karahin sab priti.* Gods, men and saints, the practice is the same; self-interest is behind their loyalty.

Survival of a pluralist society in a federal republic demands accommodation and satisfaction of all diverse elements and dangerous experiments like Emergency may give rise to the forces of disintegration. Authoritarianism and regimentation can't be forced on a society of divergent religions, languages, castes and creeds. In a democracy devoid of strong rule of law even a small unlawful can throttle the voice of the disciplined majority and even the intelligentsia choose silence as the better part of valour. Our Constitution has far greater institutional strength but moral and ideological strength of those responsible to maintain it is doubtful.

4

BUMPS AND PITFALLS

The tragic assassination of Indira Gandhi did not end Nehru-Gandhi dynasty. Believing that only another Nehru-Gandhi could steer the country out of the prevailing crisis, the Congress party unanimously elected Rajiv Gandhi to succeed his mother and he was sworn in as Prime Minister of the Republic of India on 31 October 1984 at the age of 40.

Rajiv Ratna Gandhi had never shown any interest in politics and was sincerely reluctant to join it. Assassination of his mother, explosion of communal violence that followed and the death of his elder brother, Sanjay Gandhi, paved way for his elevation and threw him in the political arena much against his wishes. He had practically no experience of political life and had never been groomed for the same by his mother. His major qualification was a youthful image and a flawless reputation as "Mr. Clean". Unlike the normal home-spun *khadi* clad professional politicians, Rajiv Gandhi was more sincere, transparent, introvert and shy by nature.

Rajiv Gandhi was married to Sonia, an Italian citizen, who had gone to Cambridge to study English where Rajiv was enrolled for his engineering degree. He was so impressed by her beauty that he penned down a piece of poetry on a napkin when he first met her at a restaurant where she was working as a part-time waitress. Sonia was also reluctant to his taking over the reins of the country. She feared that he too would be killed like his mother. Discarding personal safety and advice of his wife, Rajiv Gandhi accepted the challenge and the command of his party. His elevation is again an ample testimony to the absence of inner-party democracy in Congress party and the reluctance of the dynasty to allow any one from outside the dynasty to hold the reins of the party or those of the government.

In the elections that followed, sympathy wave became the main vote-catching potential. In a House of 543, Congress won 415, a record never achieved before or since then. Immediately after resuming office of Prime Minister, Rajiv Gandhi faced nationwide riots against the members of Sikh community due to the assassination of Indira Gandhi. His first task was to quell riots and restore confidence among the Sikhs. Another crisis that he had to face was Bhopal Gas Leak tragedy in which thousands were affected and over 2,000 had lost their lives.

To defuse the smouldering situation in Punjab and with the object of healing the wounds of the Sikhs, Rajiv Gandhi immediately ordered enquiry into the riots in

Delhi and other places. He signed an agreement with Akali Dal in July 1985 by which Chandigarh was given to Punjab. The accord, however, was put in cold storage due to fear of defeat in Haryana.

Sikh separatists again began to fortify the Golden Temple and Rajiv Gandhi was forced to order 'Operation Black Thunder' and impose President's rule in Punjab. He also tried to defuse the crisis in Assam by reaching out an accord with the major warring groups in August 1985 on the influx of Bengali-speaking immigrants who had reduced Assamese to a minority in their own state. Peace was also made with agitating guerrillas of Mizoram by bringing them into the folds of democracy.

Rajiv Gandhi's education and cultural affinity had made him more westward. An admirer of western technology, he adopted measures to introduce modern technology and took dramatic steps to take the nation to the twenty-first century. He spearheaded India's computerisation programme and every district of the country was connected with Central Government through a computer network. Science and technology were applied to missions of drinking water, literacy, health of children and pregnant women, milk production, and telephonic communication. With him also started the era of personal computers, satellite communication and multi-media education. Economic growth that was hovering around the barrier of 3-3.5 rose to 5.5.

More out of compulsion of lack of any experience than to affirm his faith in the federal principles of the Constitution, Rajiv Gandhi, unlike his mother, did not usurp all authority in his hands and tried to leave the day-to-day implementation of policies to others. He found it easier to work with young people of his generation, shunted out old time-servers and brought fresh professionals from private sector.

Rajiv Gandhi took upon war footing some of the deficiencies in *Panchayati Raj*. A plan was drafted to provide reservation of 30% seats to women but the amendment failed to get necessary legislation passed in Rajya Sabha. He also initiated Jawahar *Rozgar Yojna* to provide employment to at least one member of every poor family in villages for 80 days in a year. The concept was later on evolved into National Employment Guarantee Scheme. He introduced New Education Policy and focused on providing free good quality modern education to talented children predominantly from rural areas by establishing residential schools in each district. He was acutely aware of the issue of environmental sustainability and a new ministry of environment was created and environment clearance made mandatory for all big projects. Anti-defection law was passed in January 1985 to deal with the tendency of elected representatives to cross the floor and to discourage them from changing their party allegiance for inducement of cash and other political or non-political concessions. He thus launched a vitriolic attack on the "culture of corruption" that had become so pervasive.

Rajiv Gandhi tried to venture some economic reforms that strengthened his position but soon politics began to overpower performance. National interests were subordinated and minorities pleased at the expense of basic democratic principles. In a case of alimony for Shah Bano from her husband, Supreme Court decided in her favour. Rajiv Gandhi wilted under pressure of narrow-minded clergy and cynical outrage of Muslim orthodoxy. "The Muslim Women's (Protection of Rights upon Divorce) Act" was enacted in 1986 placing Muslim women outside the purview of country's civil code. By this pampering, weak-willed Rajiv Gandhi sacrificed broader national interests and an opportunity to strengthen right to equality was lost due to narrow and short-term political gains. His action drew sharp criticism and eroded his image of a 'modern man', says Pranab Mukherjee. The policy of appeasement of minorities that encourages divisions in the society at the cost of national interests is still on the top agenda of the dwindling Congress party. Pluralism is a dangerous factor in weakening democracy in India and divisive forces may further affect the safety of Indian democracy.

To offset losses in state assemblies he attempted to play 'Hindu card'. In August 14, 1989 judgment Supreme Court had ruled that no parties or groups could disturb the status quo of Babri Masjid, a sixteenth century mosque in Ayodhya (UP), believed to have been built by a governor of Babur by demolishing a temple built on the birthplace of Lord Ram. To please the Hindu sentiments, indecisive and confused Rajiv Gandhi came to an agreement with *Vishwa Hindu Parishad* (VHP) to proceed with a ceremony to lay foundation stone of Ram *Janmabhoomi* on a property adjacent to Babri Masjid that was not in dispute. Later on, to demonstrate his concern for Muslims, he prevented the start of work on the temple thus enraging people from both the religions. Opening of Ram *Janmabhoomi* temple site was perhaps another error of judgment, says Pranab Mukherjee in his memoir, 'The Turbulent Years: 1980-96'.

Rajiv Gandhi's handling of the religious issues was immature and he took more anti-secular decisions than any other government. By appeasing Hindus on one side and Muslims on the other, Rajiv's silly secularism encouraged consolidation of both Hindu and Muslim communal forces.

Rajiv Gandhi failed to understand the Indian way of conducting politics and did not make any effort to maintain personal touch with the masses. He himself candidly admitted that his biggest problem had been his failure to communicate with the people. In his presidential address to Congress centenary celebrations in 1985, he said, "…we have shrunk, losing touch with the toiling millions…we are a party of social transformation, but in our preoccupation with governance we are drifting away from the people."

Economic liberalisation was soon put on the back burner and resources earmarked for providing clean drinking water and electricity to the villages were diverted towards the purchase of arms due to pressure of vested political interests discarding the national policies. He said, "…we obey no discipline, no rule, follow no principle of public morality, display no sense of social awareness, show no concern for the public weal…" He admitted that government servants instead of serving the people oppressed the poor and helpless. "There can be no protection if the fence starts eating the crop." The old guards could not digest such pungent remarks. The era of decline of Congress, which started during the time of Indira Gandhi, could not be arrested by Rajiv and further declined. Unlike his mother, Rajiv Gandhi was less fortunate in inspiring the people with memorable quotes and inspirational slogans. He is blamed for turning the country into a 'banana republic'. To find the right combination of ministers of commitment, competence and integrity, he reshuffled his Cabinet no less than 26 times during his five years in office.

In an effort to strengthen capability of defence forces, and arm them with latest weapons, Rajiv Gandhi government signed a contract of USD 285 million with Swedish arms company Bofors for procuring 155mm howitzer field gun for Indian army. Subsequently Swedish

Radio alleged that Bofors paid millions of dollars as illegal commission to top Indian politicians and key defence officials through middlemen to secure the contract. The scam triggered nationwide agitation for enquiry and turned out to be the death-knell of Rajiv's political career. Few other allegations of kickbacks also emerged over the purchase of submarines from West Germany and the opposition mounted an agitation demanding his resignation.

Bofors tarnished Rajiv's otherwise clean image. Slogans of *'Gali gali mein shor hai/Rajiv Gandhi chor hai'* and *'Dus mein naun beiman/phir bhi mera Bharat mahan'* began to resound throughout the country. Rajiv Gandhi himself admitted, "Corruption is not only tolerated but even regarded as the hallmark of leadership."

Electoral debacle in many states further damaged Rajiv Gandhi's image and leaders, very close to him, left the party to join opposition parties. General elections to Lok Sabha were ordered in November 1989. Socialists once again united as Janta Dal, and Bofors, terrorism in Punjab, mishandling of Liberation Tigers of Tamil Eelam (LTTE) problem, and Nehruvian concept of socialism became the main issues at the polls.

Rajiv Gandhi lost power in 1989 and Congress, even though the single largest party, refused to form a government. National Front with the outside support of BJP and Left parties took reins of the government with rebel Congress leader VP Singh as Prime Minister.

Coalition government of VP Singh did not last long and Chandra Shekhar formed government with the backing of Congress. It lasted only a few months and elections to Lok Sabha were ordered in May 1991.

Prime Minister is an integral part of the process of elections and becomes a vulnerable target in rallies and processions. Rajiv Gandhi threw all safety precautions to the wind during one such campaign on 21 May 1991 at Sriperumbudur, 40 km from Madras. A young Tamil woman, Dhanu, armed with explosives strapped to her waist, sneaked into the crowd and exploded her treasure on the pretext of garlanding Rajiv Gandhi. The blast instantly shattered him into pieces along with the assassin and at least 20 more people.

Main cause of the conspiracy of Rajiv Gandhi assassination was sending Indian Peace Keeping Force (IPKF) at the request of Sri Lankan government to fight insurgents in a foreign country and was gravely resented by Sinhalese and Tamilians both in Sri Lanka and in India. LTTE which had harboured grievance against Rajiv Gandhi was suspected of masterminding his killing. Rajiv Gandhi was impulsive in taking political decisions, and Longowal accord in Punjab and Bodoland in Assam were other examples.

Contemporary history writing in India is poor and the accounts available are often politically motivated or written to settle personal scores. Most of the facts are taken to the grave making it difficult for historians to arrive at the truth. K. Ragothaman, chief investigating officer of Rajiv Gandhi assassination case, has alleged in his book, 'Conspiracy to kill Rajiv Gandhi – From CBI Files' that "The assassin gang as per our investigation was very much in the sterile zone for more than two and a half hours waiting for its target." The vital piece of evidence on a video tape, according to him, had been "suppressed" to spare the Tamil Nadu police and the Congress party in the middle of Lok Sabha election. RD Pradhan who was Union home secretary writes in his book, 'My Years With Rajiv and Sonia', "There is no doubt in my mind that a 'mole' from the LTTE had found refuge in 10 Janpath." He also believes that "truth shall not come out" though someone inside 10 Janpath provided crucial information to the mole. Narasimha Rao government constituted Special Investigation Team (SIT) in 1995 but the case was "buried".

Assassinations of Indira and Rajiv could not shake the solid foundations of Indian democracy. Rajiv Gandhi tried to level the path of Indian democracy so dangerously dug during Emergency by his mother but failed to strengthen the democratic institutions and the path continued to remain uneven, bumpy and slippery.

5

THROUGH NARROW LANES

Democracy bestowed its blessings on Indira Gandhi but unfortunately, she squandered it due to her vanity and tarnished its fair name. A negative vote swept the country and people emphatically voted against her for the restoration of democracy. A mega sympathy wave in the wake of her assassination catapulted an inexperienced Rajiv to prime minister's chair with a historic majority. He also showed scant respect to the verdict of the people and in almost a repeat show, was ousted 12 years later in 1989 over Bofors. On both occasions, nature of the verdict was decisively negative, with the electorate throwing out in rage leaders with unacceptable records in governance. Democracy faced grave crisis but successfully survived.

Within hours of the assassination of Rajiv Gandhi the leadership was offered to his wife Sonia Gandhi fearing losing elections unless led by someone from Nehru-Gandhi dynasty, again sacrificing democratic principles. She politely refused but soon overcame her reluctance and accepted the power. She, however, remained behind the scene and preferred to be a king-maker, a position that she continued to occupy with greater strength.

An era of alliances of convenience started with the death of Rajiv Gandhi. Last decade of 20th century witnessed four general elections, eight prime ministers and perhaps twice that number of coalition changes endangering the smooth path of Indian democracy. Congress suffered in elections in 1991 due to decline in its popularity and formed the first minority government under PV Narasimha Rao, an accidental prime minister. He was India's first prime minister outside Nehru-Gandhi family to complete five-year term without a majority in the Parliament. Democracy survived again as it had survived in earlier calamities.

Narasimha Rao was calm and quiet by nature. He was not considered a threat to anyone in the Congress party. The story of Rao's choice as prime minister is also quite dramatic. According to an account, on the advice of the long-time family confidant PN Haksar, Sonia Gandhi first invited then Vice-president Shankar Dayal Sharma who expressed his inability on grounds of age and health. Jyoti Basu's name was then suggested to Sonia that she declined. Haksar then suggested PV Narasimha Rao who had been loyal to Indira Gandhi. He was a seasoned politician and had been chief minister of Andhra Pradesh. Earlier he had managed with distinction ministries of external affairs and home under Indira, and defence and human resource development under Rajiv.

Rao was a shrewd and calculating career politician and mature in politics. Haksar and Sonia both failed to anticipate that this trustworthy ally once placed in the top office might become his own master. While Sonia's instincts in case of Manmohan Singh, also fiercely loyal to the family, proved right, those of Haksar about Rao proved wrong.

Sonia Gandhi wasn't very fond of Narasimha Rao and his elevation was considered only a stopgap arrangement. She was upset with Rao because the trial of Rajiv Gandhi assassination was moving at a very slow pace though Rao had explained to her the legal difficulties in hastening the trial. He once remarked, "I can take on Sonia Gandhi. But I do not want to do so."

Hesitant in the beginning, Rao surprised his detractors by ushering in the biggest revolution in India since 1947. He pushed through liberalisation and carried out drastic economic reforms. If Nehru gave the country a vibrant democracy, Rao paved way for modern economy. His tenure is the dividing line between old and modern India and he may be called the "development" prime minister.

In a television address on June 22, only a day after he took the oath of office, Narasimha Rao announced the broad framework of his new policy. He said, "We are determined to address the problems of economy in a decisive manner...A time-bound programme will be worked out to streamline our industrial policies and programmes to achieve the goal of a vibrant economy that rewards creativity, enterprise and innovativeness." He declared that his "government is committed to removing the cobwebs that come in the way of industrialisation." He declared to make India internationally competitive, welcome foreign direct investment to accelerate the tempo of development, upgrade technology and promote exports. His new economic reforms model was LPG that stood for liberalisation, privatisation and globalisation.

When Narasimha Rao became prime minister, economy was in a miserable mess. Foreign exchange reserves had dwindled to a dangerous level and it was only $ 1 billion in June 1991 which was just sufficient to cover only two weeks of imports. Rao understood delicacy of the situation and entered into negotiations with international financial institutions to overcome the balance of payment crisis. Domestic inflation had already reached the glaring figure of 16% in August 1991. Industrial growth was disrupted and exports had declined. To steer the economy out of this crisis, he decided to abandon some of the outdated and irrational policies of the past and for this he wanted to have an able and trustworthy finance minister. He did not trust a politician and appointed Dr. Manmohan Singh, a soft-spoken economist, knowledgeable both on the working of international financial institutions and policy making process at home.

Loan from IMF was necessary to help the government to overcome balance of payment crisis. Gold reserves were flown to London to provide collateral against $2.2

billion emergency loan. Even though the intentions were noble, it was a grave psychological shock and humiliation since gold was considered a symbol of national pride. Simultaneously, rupee was devalued in July 1991 by 20% in two steps within a period of three days. Export subsidy was abolished and exporters were given incentive through some cheaper rupee. Surprisingly, these most structured reforms were discussed with commerce minister, Palaniappan Chidambaram and commerce secretary, Montek Singh Ahluwalia, another eminent economist, and finalised only within a space of few hours.

The slow pace of decision making of the past was given an accelerating push by these four courageous revolutionaries. It amply proved that bureaucracy, often blamed to be obstructive, is highly disciplined if there is clarity and support from the top politicians. However, for currency convertibility, Manmohan Singh was unwilling and rupee is still not free from capital account. It is an irony of fate that the majority governments of Congress failed while the minority government of Rao changed the course of India's entire economic policy.

Challenges are an invitation to progress and crisis is the genesis of opportunities. Reforms of 1991 sprang from a series of back-to-the-wall measures prompted by conditions imposed by International Monetary Fund, as it forced the government into economic liberalisation. Once the crisis was over, pressure for reforms diminished and pace of reforms slowed down. Public sector was bleeding Indian economy with bankruptcy and nil production but implementation of privatisation was not enforced. Labour reforms could not be introduced and laying-off even a single worker was not possible due to political pressure and threats by trade-unions. Rao's reluctance to privatisation of public sector is evident from his statement that he "never wished to reverse the past". Again, he said, "You don't strangulate a child to whom you have given birth." Powerful farm lobby and pressure from the Left prevented abolition or even reduction of subsidies though they were increasingly eating away the financial health of the country and creating high fiscal deficit. This adversely affected growth of infrastructure and delayed reforms in health and education sectors. Even though License Raj was abolished, the Inspector Raj continued to create hurdles for the growth of industry. In spite of some bold steps in economic reforms, Rao was still a "reluctant liberaliser". After 1994, reforms became painfully slow and moved at snail pace.

With all the bold economic reforms of Narasimha Rao, some worshipers of Nehru-Gandhi dynasty deny their credit to him on the ground that all these promises had been made by Rajiv Gandhi in the 1991 Congress manifesto and Rao simply implemented them. Supporters of Rao argue that promises made in manifestos are seldom honoured and regard Rao as the architect of modern Indian economy. They sadly point out absence of even a single national monument dedicated to him only because he was not from the prestigious dynasty. He was even denied his due honours as prime minister by the Congress party on his death and Sonia Gandhi or any other Congress leader did not visit his residence on his demise. Ego of the Congress president is in fact a sign of shallow political thinking. All this was due to dynastic feudalism of Nehru-Gandhi dynasty that has been mainly responsible for its sharp decline in politics and popularity.

Narasimha Rao demonstrated that if determined, even ignorant can work wonders and create revolutionary changes. He was a political lightweight in the Congress and lacked a Lok Sabha majority. Unable to continue more radical reforms, his limited reforms broke some key binding constraints and paid miraculous dividend. It shows that even partial, inconsistent reforms can achieve a lot provided they break shackles that chain them.

Besides economic reforms, Narasimha Rao was very keen to make India a strong atomic nation. APJ Abdul Kalam, who went on to be President of India and was then a scientist at Indian Space Research Organisation (ISRO), has revealed an incident of May 1996. "It was 9 o'clock. I got a call…that I should meet Prime Minister PV Narasimha Rao immediately". Rao told Kalam to be ready and wait for the authorisation of the Prime Minister for nuclear test. However, the plan could not be implemented as the election results did not favour Rao and he then arranged a meeting of Kalam with PM-designate Atal Bihari Vajpayee. Kalam says that Rao's act of ensuring continuity of the nuclear programme, "reveals the maturity and professional excellence of a patriotic statesman who believed that the nation is bigger than the political system." Pokhran tests were finally carried out in May 1998 by Atal Bihari Vajpayee government.

Managing majority in minority government of coalitions is a great diplomatic art which Rao skillfully managed with the help of his then parliamentary affairs minister, Vidya Charan Shukla within permissible inducements under parliamentary system to ensure his government lasting its full term. He saved the government on various occasions but most crucially in the no-confidence motion of June 1992. MPs were bribed to secure their votes on the floor of the House during a trust vote. The inducements worked wonders and in a high-voltage drama, the government finally sailed through. Some investigations of political favours and monetary inducements were conducted but Shukla and other conspirators easily escaped. The dangerous path of dishonest methods, including horse-trading, and "kidnapping" was thus laid for future for the survival of coalitions which has been skillfully used several times to manage survival at the centre as well as in the states with no regard to ethical and moral values or interest of the nation. A couple of decades later, a chief minister of Delhi shed his morals and justified his unconstitutional deed of luring six Congress MLAs to secure their support by terming it as not 'horse- trading' but only "political realignment". By this logic, communalism can be termed as "religious realignment", corruption as "currency realignment", bribery as "favour realignment", adultery as "marital realignment" and every vice as "realignment" of two or more evils.

Rao's achievements of economic reforms were shadowed by another significant event that adversely affected the secular principles of the Constitution. Religious tolerance has been the hallmark of Indian ethos for ages but it is only a few fundamentalists who fan the fire of communalism and create divisions that encourage riots and separatist tendencies. One such incident that created communal disharmony and strong ill-feeling between Hindus and Muslims during the regime of Narasimha Rao was the demolition of Babri Masjid at Ayodhya. According to Pranab Mukherjee, the demolition of Babri Masjid was "senseless, wanton destruction of a religious structure, purely to serve political ends…It destroyed India's image as a tolerant, pluralist nation."

Conflict on Babri Masjid has a long history but the present problem started on the night of December 22-23, 1949 when an idol of Ram Lalla "mysteriously" appeared inside the mosque. Since mid-1980s, VHP started campaigning to 'liberate' Ram *Janambhoomi,* demolish the mosque and rebuild a temple there. The issue polarised votes on religious lines and BJP adopted it as its poll-agenda in 1990.

On the morning of December 7, 1992 about 60 *karsevaks* started assembling near Babri Masjid with rods to demolish it. It is believed that top BJP leaders, besides

Narasimha Rao, were aware of the plan. The demolition unleashed large-scale countrywide riots and about 3000 people lost their lives. The incident gave rise to an era of polarisation and Congress government at the centre was blamed for its inaction. After decades of judicial wrangling Supreme Court in a unanimous judgment in November 2019 cleared the way for the construction of a Ram Temple at the disputed site at Ayodhya and directed the Centre to allot a 5-acre plot to Suni Waqf Board for building a mosque. The construction of Ram Temple started in June 2020.

Besides many other achievements, Narasimha Rao government is also credited with the passing of Panchayati Raj Constitutional Amendment Bill. The bill was first introduced by Rajiv Gandhi government in Lok Sabha but could not be passed in Rajya Sabha. The idea was to establish "democracy at the grassroots level" and make *Panchayats* more responsible to the people. Along with this also came the 74th amendment which established local self-governments for towns and cities with no less than one-third of total seats in each tier to be reserved for women besides reservations for SCs and STs. Despite all these significant reforms Congress lost in 1996 general elections.

PV Narasimha Rao, whose tenure as PM will be better known for ushering in economic reforms and for demolition of Babri Masjid, faced several judicial hurdles once he ceased to be PM. Most serious of cases was when a special court convicted him in 2000, along with Cabinet colleague Buta Singh, for conspiring to bribe MPs from JMM, among others, to vote for his government in a no-confidence motion in 1993. The duo was sentenced to three years rigorous imprisonment and fine of rupees one lakh by trial court but both were acquitted by Delhi high court. Harshad Mehta who created a boom in the stock market also claimed to have bribed Rao.

In another case, Lakhubhai Pathak, a UK based 'pickle king', accused Rao of having promised in 1983 to get a contract supply of paper pulp and newsprint in return for pay-off to Rao, godman Chandraswami and his associate Mamaji. He alleged that while Chandraswami was paid $100,000, Rao did not keep his end of the bargain. The lower court concluded that there was enough evidence to proceed against Rao and Delhi high court upheld the same. In December 2003, Rao, Chandraswami and Mamaji were acquitted six years after Pathak's death.

In St. Kitts Forgery case in which Rao was alleged to have forged some documents to implicate former Prime Minister VP Singh and his son Ajeya Singh for having an account in a bank in the Caribbean island, the trial court discharged Rao in June 1997 for lack of evidence. It is also believed that some of these cases were politically motivated as Narasimha Rao government had set up a committee "to take stock of all information about the activities and links of mafia organisations/elements."

Narasimha Rao, the man who initiated India's liberalisation, died in utter oblivion. His greatest misfortune was that he did not belong to Nehru-Gandhi dynasty but as a shrewd politician he publicly characterised his reforms as an extension of the policies of Nehru, Indira and Rajiv thereby gaining the support of his critics and internal adversaries in Congress. In 1992 in a large public rally he described himself as the "development prime minister of India" and his policies as "complete U-turn without seeming to be U-turn". Through sheer grit and far-sightedness, the lack-luster seventy-year-old intellectual turned the forty-year old socialist legacy of his party ancestors. His political courage and tough aggressive decisions are commendable though contribution of Manmohan Singh and Chidambrum cannot be minimised. Manmohan Singh could not push such reforms as prime minister during his two tenures but still remains the chief architect of the economic reforms of 1991. It shows that political will is the key factor in any reform. Heading a minority government, Rao managed the dissent deftly like a shrewd politician only through a determined political will while Manmohan Singh with a majority government could not move even a pebble in ten years of his premiership.

The wide path of Indian democracy was laid with mud and clay of socialism which could not take load of even light economic reforms necessary for the growth of a vibrant democracy. No serious attempt was made for over four decades to mend the path and introduce significant social and economic reforms leaving the poor and down-trodden to their fate. Health and education, so vital for any developing democracy, received the least attention and in fact deliberate effort was made by the politicians to keep the people illiterate for their electoral gain. Narasimha Rao made sincere efforts to level the path to a great extent but it still remained full of pot holes.

6

MENDING THE COURSE

Another turbulent era of growing political uncertainty started in Indian democracy in 1996. In the elections that followed, no single party could win majority at the Centre. BJP emerged as the largest party but National Democratic Alliance (NDA) government with Atal Bihari Vajpayee as prime minister failed to muster enough strength from other parties and his government survived only 13 days. To avoid another BJP-led alliance, Congress extended outside support to United Front government led by HD Deve Gowda, chief minister of Karnataka, who lost the vote of confidence due to "treacherous friends". A fierce succession battle erupted and IK Gujral, a freak case and Delhi veteran was sworn in as prime minister. He was a mild-mannered, Left-leaning liberal who headed a rickety coalition that was chronically crisis-ridden, very often being rushed into intensive care. During his tenure, he masterminded the "Gujral Doctrine", advocating unilateralism in India-Pakistan affairs that lessened a bit the distrust between the two squabbling nations. Report of Jain Commission about Rajiv Gandhi assassination indicted DMK and the Congress asked the government for its removal. Gujral refused to oblige and resigned on 28 November 1997. Mid-term polls were held in February 1998 but no party or alliance could muster majority and Atal Bihari Vajpayee formed a coalition government.

It was now clear that days of single-party rule were over and governments at the centre could only be formed with the help of regional parties who could never evolve a common national approach or programme and could not rise above regional and ethnic considerations.

Atal Bihari Vajpayee realised that an insecure nation is not capable of progress. He decided in favour of the resumption of nuclear tests and his government conducted five underground nuclear tests, called Pokhran II, in May 1998, just one month after coming to power. Unlike the fiercely stubborn attitude of Congress in future to stall every programme of BJP, Sonia Gandhi on this occasion remarked, "The nuclear question is a national matter… On this, every Indian stands united."

Vajpayee was very keen to improve relations with Pakistan and in late 1998 he began full-scale diplomatic peace process. Historic inauguration of Delhi-Lahore bus service, boosting trade and Lahore Declaration with Nawaz Sharif, Prime Minister of Pakistan, committed the two nations to restore bilateral relations through dialogue. However, the Lahore Agreement's success was disturbed by the outbreak of Kargil War just months later. Indian forces launched Operation Vijay and after three-month long war, victory of Kargil hailed Vajpayee as a strong leader.

Vajpayee government collapsed on 17 April, 1999 due to coalition compulsions when Vajpayee refused to yield to the ambitious demands of AIADMK party chief, J Jayalalithaa. He said, "I have never compromised on principles in pursuit of power…" The government lost vote of confidence by a single vote and Vajpayee decided to go to the people for a fresh mandate.

In the elections of 1999, BJP emerged as the largest party and could form a government with the help of its allies. A cohesive block of 13 parties of competing interests joined BJP and Vajpayee was sworn in as prime minister of India for the third time on 13 October 1999. He was the first non-Congress prime minister to serve full term from October 1999 to May 2004. It was during this tenure that Vajpayee introduced many economic and infrastructural reforms and promoted pro-business free market reforms to boost economy initiated by Narasimha Rao.

India's two great reformist prime ministers were PV Narasimha Rao and Atal Bihari Vajpayee. Both were not free market ideologues but realised that key to prosperity lay in rolling back the overbearing role of government in economy, and correcting errors of Nehru and Indira Gandhi that kept India economically backward. Both these reformist PMs did not belong to the dynasty and generated prosperity by dismantling Nehruvian contention of mistrust of trade, contempt for profit motive, and faith in state planning rather than in the market. Whereas Rao chose to maintain a defensive posture on reforms, often describing them as a continuation of Nehru-Gandhi era policies, Vajpayee propagated them proactively and expanded the process of economic liberalisation initiated by Rao. Rao had scrapped industrial licencing, slashed trade tariffs, made room for the private sector in areas once walled off by government, and Vajpayee effectively took the baton from him and ran even faster. Vajpayee was a man of firm political conviction and a man of the masses unlike Rao.

UPA's record on corruption disgusted the nation but BJP was also not free from this menace. In March 2001, Tehelka group released a sting operation named Operation West End showing videos of BJP President Bangaru Laxman, senior army officers and NDA members accepting bribes from journalists posing as agents and businessmen. Defence Minister George Fernandes was forced to resign following the Barak Missile scandal involving the botched supplies of coffins for soldiers killed in Kargil and findings of an inquiry commission that the government could have prevented Kargil invasion.

Another significant event damaged the reputation of Vajpayee government. On December 24, 1999, five hijackers stormed the cockpit of Kathmandu-Delhi Indian Airlines flight IC-814 with 179 passengers including

11 crew members on board when it was over Lucknow. The hijackers took the plane t0 Amritsar for fuel and then to Lahore. The plane was then hijacked by Rauf Azhar and his associates to Kandhar. The government wilted under public pressure and the passengers were released on December 31, 1999 in exchange for three dreaded terrorists, one of them being Azhar Masood, brother of Rauf Azhar. Decision to release the three terrorists was supported by all major parties, including Congress, for the safe security of the passengers. Former External Affairs Minister Jaswant Singh, who took the ridiculous and disgraceful decision of accompanying the three freed terrorists, has defended the government decision to save lives of hijacked passengers. Azhar Masood went on to establish Jaish-e-Mohammed, one of the terrorist groups that has constantly created problems for Indian forces in Kashmir. He has also been implicated in the Mumbai terror attack.

Vajpayee government has been blamed for being "soft on terror" and indirectly helping laying the "foundation of terrorism" for which the nation is paying heavy price. Critics blame the government for shameful sacrifice of vital national interests and claim that the government "frittered away opportunities to gun down terrorists" when the flight landed at Amritsar and stayed there for 49 minutes. Congress government did the same in 1991 and released nine militants to secure the release of an executive director of Indian Oil kidnapped by militants in Srinagar. Two years later, nearly four dozen

JKLF militants were allowed safe passage by the Congress government from Hazratbal shrine where they had held 170 people hostages for six weeks. On 13 December 2001, a group of masked armed men with fake IDs stormed the Parliament House in Delhi. This attack, led by Lashkar-e-Taiba and Jaish-e-Mohammad, resulted in the death of a dozen people but the security forces killed all attackers who were later proven to be Pakistani nationals. As a result of this, Prevention of Terrorism Act was promulgated by the NDA government which gave wide authority to government to crack down and hold anybody. Government had to face vigorous opposition of non-NDA parties and the Act was also condemned by Human Rights groups. Cross border terrorism had started showing dangerous signs but the world community failed to show any serious concern to combat the rising terrorism. All Indian governments and various political parties have also been soft towards terrorists and parties in opposition have never displayed unity towards such a vital national issue which is a dangerous signal for the growth and welfare of democracy. Absence of a unified national strength has been the greatest weakness of India and a vital cause of her centuries of slavery.

In his sincere effort to maintain friendly relations with Pakistan, Vajpayee again broke the ice in 2001. He invited Pakistan President Parvez Musharraf, the man who had planned Kargil invasion, for a joint summit and peace talks that failed to achieve a breakthrough as Musharraf declined to leave aside the issue of Kashmir.

On the 10th anniversary of Babri mosque demolition, VHP wanted to perform '*shila daan*', ceremony laying the foundation stone of the cherished temple at the disputed site. Tens of thousands of VHP activists gathered and threatened to overrun the site and forcibly build the temple. The government was, however, able to tide over the crisis rather smoothly. Vajpayee could not resolve the Ram *Janmabhoomi* dispute, repealing Article 370, which gave a special status to the state of Jammu and Kashmir, or enacting a Uniform Civil Code owing to lack of coalition support.

Working under compulsions of coalition politics, Vajpayee always kept himself clear of personal and political ambitions. He never let caste politics and anti-secular forces sway his judgment. His tenure is, however, tarnished with anti-Muslim riots in Gujarat in April 2002. The rioting began at Godhra, a small town in Gujarat where 58 Hindu *karsevaks* returning from Ayodhaya were put to death in a fire that engulfed a compartment of the Sabarmati Express. This provoked retaliation and wide spread riots in many cities of Gujarat. The riots left 2000 dead and about two lakh homeless due to large-scale exodus from villages. Vajpayee publicly criticised these anti-Muslim riots but the government was blamed for failing to control and quell the violence.

Vajpayee's foreign policy was praiseworthy. It was during his tenure that American President Bill Clinton visited India in March 2000 and relations between India and US improved considerably. Trade and economic ties were strengthened and Historic Vision Document was signed. Vajpayee also launched the '*Pravasi Bhartiya Samman*' for Non-Resident Indians and initiated plans to establish an overseas citizenship of India to enable NRIs to invest and do business freely in India. He remarked, "To reform is to turn the inevitability of change in the direction of progress". Vajpayee also tried to improve relations with China for boosting trade and resolving territorial disputes through dialogue. He visited China and recognised Tibet as a part of China. In return, China recognised Sikkim as part of India. Strategic and military cooperation was established with Israel to fight terrorism. India also provided strategic assistance to US for its war against Taliban and Al-Qaeda after 2001.

After the good show in assembly elections in four northern states, BJP decided to seek premature dissolution of the 14th Lok Sabha. The economy was believed to be doing well. There seemed to be no clear anti-incumbency and BJP decided to capitalise on "India Shining" slogan. Although no single party won a clear majority, Congress bagged slightly more seats than BJP and formed the UPA government under Manmohan Singh with the coalition of the regional parties.

The path of Indian democracy that had been leveled a bit by Narasimha Rao was made further smooth by Vajpayee due to his far-sighted economic reforms and pragmatic international diplomacy. Nehruvian socialism got further jolt by liberalising trade, reducing pressure of Licence Raj and encouraging foreign investment. It is an irony of fate that non-economists successfully brought economic reforms while the expert and renowned economist failed to strengthen the Indian economy in the next one decade. It proves that it is the will and determination to progress that is paramount and not mere talent or intelligence.

7

THROUGH CHAMBAL VALLEY

With the advent of UPA after NDA, democracy passed through upheavals of scams and democratic institutions began to suffer deep dents. The key person who played a vital role, directly or behind the scenes, in Indian politics in the coming decade was Sonia Gandhi. In his memoirs, 'One Life Is Not Enough', Natwar Singh says that Sonia's life can be divided into four phases. First, three were era of matrimonial bliss, wife of a prime minister, and life of seclusion from 1991 to 1998 when she rejected all offers to join politics. The fourth phase began on 14 March 1998, when she formally took over as Congress President and remained in that position for fifteen years, longest in the history of Congress. According to him, she is neither a communicator nor an orator. Her brain is razor sharp. She never gives away what is in her mind, is obsessively secretive and suspicious, and evokes awe and not admiration. Over the years she changed from a nervous and shy woman to an ambitious and authoritarian leader. In 1998 she was elected to Lok Sabha from Amethi but did not speak even once in her first term.

In 2004, Congress swept the polls and responsibility to form the government once again fell on the shoulders of Sonia Gandhi. Fearing fate like her mother-in-law and her husband, she offered the post of PM to Manmohan Singh. This cunning ploy suited her character to hold the reins in her hands and pull the strings whenever required without sharing any responsibility. Her style of functioning is completely devoid of democratic principles, both within the party and in the government. Natwar Singh also says that he told her that in history she and Julius Caesar are the only two people, both Italian by birth, who had refused the crown.

In the 2009 elections of Lok Sabha, Congress-led UPA once again won a comfortable majority, giving it and Manmohan Singh a second successive term. Manmohan Singh's political career had started with his election to Rajya Sabha and appointment as finance minister in Narasimha Rao government in 1991. Before that, he had been a teacher in economics at Punjab University, secretary in the department of economic affairs, Governor Reserve Bank and Chairman University Grants Commission (UGC). When Rao lost election and Sonia took over the reins of Congress party, he was quick to switch loyalty to her. He is a committed sycophant by nature and a perfect 'yes man'. As a career bureaucrat, he had always practiced loyalty to whosoever was above him and had the ability to shift loyalty with the change. If asked to choose between doing the right thing in a specific instance and pursuing the orders of his boss, even if wrong, he would and did choose the latter. To solidify Sonia's trust in him, he went so far as to publicly assert during his 1999 election campaign that Congress had played no role in the 1984 massacre of Sikhs and shifted the entire blame to RSS instead. He talked about "a mindless environment of negativism", and lack of accountability and "institutional subversion" in the country but his timidity and blind loyalty to Sonia Gandhi negated all his good qualities and blocked his intellect. He also professed that politics is the art of the possible but did little to expand the range of possibilities.

When Manmohan Singh became prime minister, there was great hope that he would focus attention on economic development and strengthen democratic institutions. Instead, he silently watched their doom as a mute spectator. His government disregarded the virtues of honesty and competence while favouring pliability and selfish political interests. The price of this systematic and willful corrosion of public institutions was paid not merely by upright individuals but by the people of India as a whole. Democratic institutions suffered grievous damages and democracy had to pass through thick jungle infested with corrupt dacoits.

There are moments in a nation's history when its leaders can make decisive turns but such moments are rare and not always easily available. Just after India's 2009 elections UPA-2 had such a great moment. The prime minister could arguably have pushed through many significant reforms despite some uncooperative coalition partners. But a tsunami of self-created scandals eroded government's credibility and encouraged a series of scams that did great damage to the democratic fabric.

Daron Acemoglu and James Robinson have written in 'Why Nations Fail' that countries lose steam because their institutions don't measure up. India also slipped up because of regulatory weakness, legislative deadlock and pressure of coalition partners. Manmohan Singh, without real political power or control over his own party, had to work with these aggressive coalition partners devoid of shame. His personal ambition to continue as PM always remained shielded behind his silence and overt humility. Still, his basic decency is admired by all and even his criticism is gently worded. He never viewed issues from the perspective of curbing wrongdoing by others. He has argued publicly that corruption grows along with economic development thereby advocating learning to live with corruption. He was personally honest but blindly tolerated corrupt people around him. He practiced active morality for himself and passive morality with respect to others and this dilemma damaged his reputation. He often said that he believes that history will treat him more kindly than contemporary media. Martin Luther King once said, "ultimate measure of a man is not where he stands in moments of comfort and convenience, but where he stands at times of challenge and controversy."

Manmohan Singh justified his bowing down to coalition partners due to blackmail by "coalition compulsions". He rewarded them for their support with loot of natural resources. Coal block allocations approved by PM has brought the row right to his doorstep. He said, "Some decisions which appear sensible ex-ante, may ex-post turn out to be faulty."

In her book "Strictly Personal, Manmohan and Gursharan", Daman Singh, Manmohan Singh's daughter defends him and says that her father is not a manipulative politician or a wheeler-dealer. She says that he believes that it is difficult to change things in India unless the system breaks down completely because in a large democracy it's only when things reach breaking point that people are willing to change the system. She also says that people will forget Manmohan Singh's failings, and remember him as the father of economic reforms and superfast growth. Guilty conscience pricks the mind and she defended him by hoping that history will be kind to him. His personal integrity has been beyond question but this provides little comfort in a venal political system. Manmohan Singh is hugely intelligent but vastly lacked determination and political will to push things through. History may not criticise him as a man but certainly as a weak prime minister for as Nehru said, "I trust that all our criticism will be based on policy and not on personalities." As finance minister he launched India's economic reforms in 1991 and as Prime Minister he presided over economic growth that halved from 9% to 4.5%, inflation averaged almost 10% for five years, and unending scams resulted in the worst-ever electoral defeat for the Congress party. Entire blame for the failures of UPA government squarely lies on Sonia Gandhi, the unquestioned ruler during the period. She cleverly managed things from behind the stage as per her desires and Manmohan Singh's unimpeachable reputation for integrity provided a safe cover to the dynasty when the scams exploded.

Sonia Gandhi did not listen to Singh's pleadings for reforms. New rules for FDI in multi-brand retail were so loaded with cumbersome clauses that they did not yield much investment. Subsidy on diesel was supposed to be phased out but crash in the rupee raised import price and diesel price remained high. Cabinet Committee on Investment cleared stuck projects worth 6 lakh crores but they did not translate into any boom for capital goods or construction contracts because of a new licence *raj* coming up. The old licence *raj* was based on industrial licences, import licences and forex controls. The new was based on environment, forests, tribal areas and land acquisition. Judicial activism made bureaucrats wary of taking any decision. "Blame is a lazy man's wages", says a proverb. Manmohan Singh attempted to pass off prime ministerial failures to the inevitable democratic compulsions of coalition government and Congress blamed the opposition for not allowing the Parliament sticking to constitutional tracks, executive not responding in an appropriate manner and legislature going beyond jurisdiction.

Political careers rarely end on a cheerful note but leaders are ultimately judged not by their failures but by their achievements. Failures of Manmohan Singh are directly attributable to Sonia Gandhi as she pulled the strings to promote her crazy schemes and the PM capitulated forgetting all the good economics he had learnt. There have been many highs like National Rural Employment Guarantee Act (NREGA), later relabeled as Mahatma Gandhi National Rural Employment Guarantee Act (MGNREGA), Protection of Women Against Domestic Violence Act, Right to Information Act, Right to Education Act, Food Security Act, Lok Pal acts, Recognition of Forests Right Act, Land Acquisition, Rehab and Resettlement Bill, Companies Bill, Women's quota bill, 8 new IITs, 7 IIMs and 30 Central Universities planned for 11th five-year plan.

Manmohan Singh, one of India's largest serving prime ministers, will go down in history as a tragic figure. For a prime minister with an uninterrupted decade in office, Singh's poor track record in ushering in administrative reforms cost India dear. There were landmark legislations passed but after taking all the positives into account, his premiership was lackluster and may be turned as a decade of squandered opportunities. India's historic nuclear deal with US is an example of disappointment. His inability or unwillingness to push his own party and bureaucracy into actualising his vision was a let-down. Quality of governance could not improve. *Aadhaar* is an example of half-hearted effort.

The institution of democracy suffered most during UPA-2 mainly due to rampant corruption, scams and scandals. Benefits of some sensible legislations were neutralised by the cases of corruption. Possible opportunities were lost mainly due to the lame excuse of compulsive coalition and fear of losing the government. National interests were sacrificed for personal and petty party interests, and no political vision was shown in implementing constructive reforms. The crippling democracy already on the rough path of bumps and pitfalls struggled to survive through the corruption-ridden jungles.

History repeats itself because we don't learn from it. In the absence of a far-sighted leader, voters rejected the Congress-led government in 2014 elections as socialist policies had proven to be the biggest poverty multiplication programmes.

In 2014 elections, while most political parties were relying on traditional caste calculations and freebee strategies to woo voters, Narendra Modi campaigned on the promise of *'Sabka saath, sabka vikas'*, most inclusive since '*garibi hatao*'. The innovative idea paid handsome dividends. He won a landslide in 2014 and 2019 on the promise of '*Achhey din aayenge*'. He is a '*chai-wallah*' who has affirmed the aspirations of millions.

Modi is clean and bold, and has taken courageous steps in the interest of the nation ignoring petty partisan interests. Law on triple *talaq* and removal of Article 370 are examples of political consciousness. Surgical strike on Pakistan and destroying the terrorist camps and hideouts right in the heart of the enemy territory is also an ample testimony of resolution of India in rooting out terrorism from the state. Policy against Chinese intrusion in Ladakh region has proved him to be a strong prime minister. Firmness against the opposition sponsored farmers' agitation opposing the most progressive laws for their future is another glaring example of his decisions in the larger interest of the nation. As a seasoned diplomat he withdrew the law and repealed it on the persistent demand of the farmers. In politics, as in war, sometimes one has to take a step or two back to strike more effectively at the right time. In spite of desperate moves of the opposition parties to weaken his efforts and of foreign forces joining hands to deprive India of becoming a global supper power, Modi has enlivened the hope of strengthening the crumbling democratic institutions.

Democracy is like a delicate plant that needs certain type of soil, climate, nutrients and care. With the type of soil available, other essentials can be provided by a strong and bold leadership who can take hard decisions for the welfare of the nation. This is becoming difficult due to corrupt politicians, uncooperative opposition, intolerant minorities, disintegration gangs, weakening federal structure, misplaced interpretations of secularism and opportunistic media. All these disruptive forces have weakened the structure of democracy but the derailed democracy is limping to come back on a smooth track.

PART – B

8

THROUGH GATES AND MARSH

The word 'corruption' is derived from Latin word *com*, meaning "with, together" and *rumpere*, meaning "to break" someone's trustworthiness and reputation with others. It is a complex phenomenon and cannot be defined by a simple definition. The World Bank has defined it as "the abuse of public power for private benefit" which is simplest. It is also improper and selfish exercise of power and influence. This great social evil is deeply embedded in the selfish and greedy nature of man and has been a part of human society since the beginning of mankind. It is one of the deadliest diseases to the health of a progressive democracy, and is a sign of political instability and institutional decay.

Historically, major part of India has been subjected to invasions and rule by outsiders during the last about one thousand years. All this has made us more selfish, self-centred, grabbers and less concerned about the care of others and welfare of the nation. After independence new global factors further strengthened the 'animal spirit'. It spread to wider political and social sectors and is now rampant in all walks of life.

Corruption is pervasive all over the world on account of capitalism and economic liberalisation. Indians have certainly greasy fingers but the glass is no cleaner on the other side. According to Transparency International Corruption Perception Index (CPI) of 2020 for 180 countries, India ranks at 86 with a score of 40 out of 100. All neighbouring countries, except Bhutan and China, rank much below India. The ranking also shows that per capita income and level of corruption are inversely proportional to each other and high-income countries tend to have lower levels of corruption.

In India, corruption was particularly wild during the tenure of UPA. Manmohan Singh's period as Prime Minister has been notorious for large scale scams and rat race to corner and grab the natural resources due to appeasement of corrupt coalition partners and failure of the ambitious-driven government to rein them.

Exploitation of natural resources like coal was one of the most favourite sources of corruption and exploitation for politicians and bureaucrats during UPA regime. Coining the term 'resource curse', British economist Richard M Auty said that countries and societies abundant in natural resources tended to be underdeveloped and had poor social indices. Natural resources are potentially big employer but corruption, cronyism and policy paralysis deprive the larger population of their benefits.

Coal is India's primary source of energy and 72% of power generated is coal-based. Jharkhand has one of the richest coal reserves of about 300 billion tone. Despite this, the country is unable to produce coal of sufficient quantity and quality leading to perennial shortage for power plants. All coal mines were nationalised in 1973 and brought under the newly formed PSU called Coal Mines Authority Limited.

Out of a spate of scams during UPA regime, 'Coalgate', often called the knight of corruption scams, was one of great significance and cost the country billions of dollars. Hundreds of coal blocks were allocated to private sector firms for captive mining without auction.

Out of the declared illegal allocations, 162 pertain to the UPA rule, 48 to the period when PM Manmohan Singh held charge of coal ministry, 7 took place under NDA government of Atal Bihari Vajpayee and the rest were made by Narasimha Rao government. CAG estimated "notional loss" of rupees 1.86 lakh crore in all these allocations. In the open bidding process later in 2014-15, the government raised 2 lakh crore through auctioning of mining rights and royalty from 30 blocks, thus breaching the CAG estimate.

In August 2014, Supreme Court declared that all the 218 coal block allocations "suffer from the vice of arbitrariness and legal flaws." The court observed that coal ministry officials and or the screening committee acted in a manner which was "detrimental" to public interest and that there had been no proper application of mind and transparency, and guidelines were seldom honoured by the screening committee. The Court was so incensed that it cancelled 214 out of 218 coal blocks terming the allotment process as "arbitrary and illegal". No compensation was paid to the honest who had invested millions and had not been found guilty of corruption, and the government guilty of wrongful coal allocations suffered no penalty. The judgment deepened fears among foreign investors about unpredictability of policies in India. The government did not take the radical step to overturn the ill-conceived policy of nationalisation and reform the ailing industry due to the stronghold of unions and vested interests of politicians and bureaucrats.

In a noteworthy verdict in May 2017, the special CBI court set up to try cases of alleged corruption in coal blocks allotment, sentenced former Jharkhand Chief Minister, Madhu Koda to three-year rigorous imprisonment and slapped a fine of rupees 25 lakh. Former coal secretary HC Gupta, former Jharkhand chief secretary and Vinay Joshi, a close associate of the ex-CM were also awarded three-year jail term and fines for corruption and criminal conspiracy. HC Gupta and two other senior IAS officers were also convicted in November 2018 for corruption in another coal block allocation. Gupta had a solid reputation for integrity and became victim of the dishonest and corrupt executive. Fear of any such later action or retaliation that may consume the honest bureaucrats result in policy paralysis. It was a travesty of justice that the screening committee of bureaucrats who were willing collaborators, conspirators and even partners with their 'political masters' was not held accountable.

In his book, 'Crusader or Conspirator? Coalgate and Other Truths', PC Parakh, who retired as coal secretary, says that in 2004, he "had pointed out that the process of allocation was leading to lobbying, pressure and windfall gain to allottees. This was brought to the notice of PM who was holding the portfolio at that time." He also says, "It is unfortunate that while the PM was keen on implementing open bidding, he was unable to counter vested interests within his government and the party." Governance, he says, cannot be sacrificed at the altar of compulsion of coalition politics but Manmohan Singh succumbed to such compulsions. This has been his greatest weakness of character.

Sanjay Baru, Manmohan Singh's media adviser has been brutally courageous. In his thoughtful book, 'The Accidental Prime Minister', he has claimed that Manmohan Singh's government was actually being run by Sonia Gandhi who was a manipulative figure behind the scenes. People often remarked that Manmohan presides and Sonia decides. Whatever the political and coalition compulsions, a prime minister of integrity must rise above petty interests and not succumb to any pressure. He should have courage to resign rather than sacrifice national interests. Martin Luther once said what aptly applies to Manmohan Singh, "You are not only responsible for what you say, but also for what you do not say." HR Bhardwaj, former law minister in the UPA government, remarked that Sonia Gandhi was "in the grip of couple of sycophants and corrupt people."

There is no doubt about the knowledge and intelligence of Manmohan Singh but these qualities alone are not enough to be on top. An honest king is also 'dishonest' if he does not exercise his power, which he possesses enormously, to check inefficiency and corruption in his kingdom. To say that Manmohan Singh was honest will be a misnomer in the context of his duties towards the nation. He was a weak prime minister who lacked courage and determination to uphold truth and maintain his loyalty to the nation. A blind king in *Mahabharta* ruined his kingdom and a blind-folded prime minister tarnished the fair name of his nation.

The fact that sustains the personal honesty of Manmohan Singh is that there is no money trail implicating him and if he presided over bad policy that does not ipso facto prove criminal misconduct. The court said that Singh acted in "complete disregard to the direction of law, rules/regulations and guidelines" to "accommodate" some in allocating coal blocks. Being in charge of coal portfolio, Singh was the "competent authority", person with whom the final decision rested. Various acts of Singh indicated his involvement in the conspiracy and the fact that he chose to keep coal portfolio with him raises questions. Parakh has also revealed that cash-strapped Air India was pushed by the then civil aviation minister, Praful Patel, to purchase Boeing 777 aircraft which were sold to Etihad within five years at one-fifth of the original price. He says that he was also under pressure to drop the name of the minister from federal auditor's report on the controversial purchase of these aircrafts. In Coalgate scam former law minister Ashwani Kumar had to resign for allegedly pressuring CBI to dilute PMO's role.

'Coalgate' investigations seem to have hit a roadblock. The case is still pending in the court and CBI is awaiting files from the coal ministry. As many as 257 files relating to coal allocation are missing from the ministry. "The disappearance and non-furnishing of documents have an element of criminality in it", remarked the court.

'Coalgate' gave birth to another scam involving companies inflating value of coal imports from Indonesia for their power plants thus siphoning money abroad to divert the same to tax havens. As a result of coal scam, iron ore mining in some states had also been shut down and Indian steel plants were forced to import iron ore. The solution is to denationalise coal mining, stop illegal mining, nail the guilty and encourage legitimate activity. Halfway measures won't work as it is no longer possible to overlook the elephant in the room.

'Spectrumgate' is another significant scam of UPA government and relates to the manner in which 2G spectrum licences were distributed. According to CAG report, this distribution was almost like gifts and the notional loss to the exchequer was estimated to be rupees 1.76 lakh crore. Telecom minister A Raja, in conspiracy with other accused, advanced the cut-off date for receiving applications to illegally favour "ineligible" firms in allocation of 2G licences.

Pradeep Baijal, former Chairman of Telecom Regulatory Authority of India (Trai), has said in his book, 'The Complete Story of Indian Reforms: 2G, Power, and Private Enterprise – A Practitioner's Diary' that Manmohan Singh appeared to be a person with a "non-economic attitude" and had a "harmful political attitude towards the economy." He also termed UPA's second term as a period of "crony capitalism" and has alleged that Manmohan Singh warned to "harm" him if he did not cooperate in the 2G case. He also claims that PM told him to cooperate in the coalition government he headed, since "non-cooperation could compromise his government."

Former comptroller and auditor general, Vinod Rai, has made damning disclosures in his book, 'Not Just An Accountant'. According to him, Prime Minister was aware of 2G spectrum scam that resulted in colossal loss to public exchequer. He has named three MPs of UPA who tried to persuade him to keep the PM's name out from the CAG report on 2G spectrum allocation. "Politicians came to my home and told me not to name some people and to protect some others in connection with the CWG and coal allocation reports." He says that there was evidence of 2G licences being given out at particular prices not only from Raja's time but before also from the previous minister Dayanidhi Maran's time who was also from DMK. His properties worth rupees 742 crore were attached by the Enforcement Directorate in March 2015 in connection with alleged Aircel-Maxis deal scam. Earlier, properties worth rupees 1,000 crore, belonging to YS Jagan Mohan Reddy, were also attached in connection with the VANPIC project scam. Vinod Rai also says that Singh had enough time to stop the allocations but "somehow it did not take place." He says, "The buck stops at the PM's desk in any parliamentary democracy", but the PM "probably chose not to stop". He also says that had the PM put his foot down "probably the fate of UPA-2 would have been different."

On February 2, 2012 Supreme Court cancelled all 122 spectrum licences allotted in January 2008 and ordered their auction within four months. However, in December, 2017 CBI court acquitted A Raja, DMK chief K Karunanidhi's daughter Kanimozhi and all others accused in the 2G spectrum scam holding that there was no criminality or conspiracy in the spectrum allotment. No appeal was filed by NDA government due to political considerations of favour from DMK for some future coalition requirements and national interest got crucified at the altar of narrow political interests. It is not only Congress that is at the root cause of such favours, no party is free from this virus. Justice is a sacrificial lamb at the altar of political favouritism. In politics democracy is twisted as per convenience and parties follow politics of gain with no regard to ethical values or welfare of the nation. It is aptly remarked that the only 'ism' that matters most in Indian politics is 'opportunism'.

Court-mandated investigation in 2G and Coalgate scams hurt the government image and corruption damaged the smooth working of democracy. Government blamed that repeated judicial interventions in economic policy affairs shook investors' confidence, leading to economic slowdown. Democratic institutions, like judiciary, provide checks and balances but a corrupt government is deliberately blind to blame and misuse these institutions. Telecom, coal and mining came under court's scanner and it could not be a mute spectator. Court interfered in decisions of the government and not in its policy framing. Instead of action to cleanse the political stable of rogue elements and check corruption by high profile politicians, the government constantly attempted to launch a concerted attack to defeat judiciary's praiseworthy work. Government did not ensure fair play and transparency that mandated judicial intervention which was not a spoke in the economic progress of the country. In rural India there is a saying, "You fall from the ass but blame the potter." Government blames judiciary but is blind to its own lapses of policies and their implementation. The

Supreme Court rightly observed in one of its judgments, "in a state where society suffers from moral denigration and simultaneously from rampant corruption, there must be an effective forum to check the same."

Scams have not been in the award of contracts for natural resources only but also in the procurement of defence equipment which is not only a national betrayal but also amounts to sacrificing country's security. The first such scam was in 1948 and is known as Jeep Scandal. VK Krishna Menon, Indian High Commissioner in Britain, who later on became India's defence minister, bypassed procurement protocols to sign a deal worth rupees 80 lakh to buy 155 jeeps from UK which, many alleged, were second hand. Defence minister, George Fernandes, had to quit after his party's treasurer boasted about collecting bribes along with Jaya Jaitley from arms dealers. Allegations emerged in 1987 that German defence firm had paid commission for the purchase of submarines.

Bofors scandal was perhaps the most infamous of all defence scandals that the country has seen. Eight years after the assassination of Rajiv Gandhi, charge sheet was filed in October 1999. He was named as one among several others who had a role in the scandal. Proclaimed offender, Ottavio Quattrocchi, an Italian close to Gandhi family, was suspected to access $1 million and Euro 3 million from the Bofors deal. UPA government had the option to press for a freeze of UK bank accounts of this controversial fugitive middleman but chose not to do so. With his death on 13th July, 2013, all accused in the rupees 64-crore kickback case have died and whole issue has now died its natural death. WikiLeaks founder Julian Assange revealed in April 2013 that Rajiv Gandhi was the "negotiator" for the Swedish jet firm Saab-Scania for Viggen. All this has been termed by Congress as "spreading lies and falsehood".

In defence deals, 'Choppergate' scam is another significant case of kickbacks. In August 1999, deal for buying 12 helicopters for replacement of Mi-8 VVIP helicopters was initiated under Vajpayee government. Technical requirements were changed in 2006 and 556 million Euro (rupees 3,546 crore) contract was signed to favour AgustaWestland, a UK based subsidiary of Italian Finmeccanica. In February 2012 Finmeccanica CEO and AW chief were arrested in Italy over allegations of unethical dealings and sentenced to 4.5 years and 4 years imprisonment. Kickbacks paid in India were suspected to be rupees 452 crore out of which rupees 414 crore came to the Indian officials, including IAF chief SP Tyagi.

'Choppergate' reveals a big nexus of middlemen and so called defence consultants who have easy access to politicians, bureaucrats and military brass in India and Italy. In April 2016, the Milan Court of Appeals blamed the Indian government (UPA-2) for not providing adequate evidence and critical documents to Italian prosecutors in 2013-14. The court also took note of documents which have accused mentioning Sonia, her political secretary Ahmed Patel and Oscar Fernandes as influential persons who could have managed the environment. The judgment has also listed a conversation where UK-based alleged middleman, Christian James Michel, who had met many politicians, bureaucrats and businessmen in this connection, identifies key members as "Manmohan Singh, Ahmed Patel, Pranab Mukherjee, M Veerappa Moily, Oscar Fernandes, MK Narayanan and Vinay Singh." According to a handwritten note supposed to have been written by Michel, the commission was allegedly distributed as "15/16m Euro marked for 'Fam'; 8.4m Euro for 'Bur' (possibly bureaucrats); 6m Euro for AF (possibly Air Force); 3m for 'AP' under 'Pol' (politicians).

In 2017 CBI filed a charge sheet against Michel who was given Euro 42 million bribe by AgustaWestland for further payments to politicians, public servants and other middlemen. He was extradited from the UAE and brought to Delhi on December 4, 2018. The tragedy is that the Indian government tried to sweep the issue under the carpet and claimed that the investigations are at an advanced stage. CBI's track record of investigations is appalling because of the government's policy to 'go slow and then stop' due to political compulsions. Veil over scams in defence acquisitions needs to be lifted as it not only leads to high cost escalations but the delay may have serious consequences in case of any eventuality. Military modernisation now looks a more likely casualty than corruption. Silence of the heavy artillery Bofors gun and empty shouts in 'Choppergate' have proved that in corruption India remains a big wasteland.

National Herald is another case of corruption, manipulated by Nehru-Gandhi family and politicians close to the family. It was a newspaper founded by Jawaharlal Nehru in 1938, published by Associated Journals Ltd, (AJL) and was popularly known as 'Voice of India'. It went temporarily out of print in 2008 and Sonia Gandhi ordered the closure of AJL in 2009. Real estate of AJL worth over rupees 2,000 crore in 7 cities was fraudulently usurped by Congress through Young Indian (YI), a company incorporated in November 2010, by paying an interest-free loan of rupees 50 lakh from the Congress party, which it could not give to a public limited company as a political party exempt from paying tax. Sonia Gandhi, Rahul Gandhi, then Congress treasurer Motilal Vora, and senior Congressman Oscar Fernandes were directors/shareholders of Young Indian with 76% equity owned by Gandhis. Subramanyam Swamy, a BJP member and a Rajya Sabha MP, smelt the rat and filed a complaint in 2014, saying that Gandhis, together with their loyalists, conspired to hijack and illegally acquire a public listed company AJL with thousands of crores of real estate via a privately managed trust YI. Both Sonia Gandhi and Rahul Gandhi were summoned to the trial court. All veteran Congress leaders reached the court in a big procession and with great funfair as a show of their strength and solidarity towards their leaders. The court granted bail to all on 19, December 2015 and observed that "serious imputations smacking of criminality" needed to be properly looked into. Congress has accused BJP government of "political vendetta". The case is limping and may meet the normal political end.

Scams and corruption cases have not been confined to UPA or centre but have been a part of all parties and states. There were six fodder scams – five in Jharkhand and one in Bihar. In January 1996, CBI court in Ranchi convicted Lalu Prasad Yadav, RJD chief and former railway minister, and 44 others for fraudulent withdrawal of rupees 37.7 crore from Chaibasa treasury using fake bills for buying fodder and medicines for cattle and Lalu Prasad was sentenced to five years in jail. Three times CM of Bihar, Jagannath Mishra, was also convicted along with four IAS officers in the same case. Lalu Prasad along with others has also been convicted, sentenced and fined in Deoghar, Doranda and other fodder scam cases. He was disqualified from contesting polls for 11 years. His conviction shows that Indian judicial system is capable of taking stringent action against politicians accustomed to immunity and is a welcome sign of democratic maturity. However, much more needs to be done against the tainted politicians to reinforce rule of law and further strengthen democratic institutions. Lack of political will and political favouritism are the root cause of slow action.

Another alleged rupee 1,000 crore scam is known as Bhagalpur Srijan scam. In 1996 Manorma Devi set up

Srijan Mahila Vikas Sahyog Samiti Limited at Ranchi. The society was to help women in small income-generating activities such as stitching, and making *bindis*, incensed sticks, *sattu* etc. In connivance with banks, government officials and Mahesh Mandal, in-charge of the treasury at Bhagalpur, she fraudulently diverted bank money to Srijan account. Mahesh Mandal was arrested but died in judicial custody after a week due to kidney failure though some alleged that he was killed to bury the truth. Manorma Devi also died in February 2017.

Saradha Group was another alleged political scandal. It was a consortium of over 200 private companies running collective investment schemes popularly referred to as chit funds. Sudipta Sen, chief of Saradha Group, embezzled about rupees 3,500 crore around 2000 through shady accounts of this ponzi scheme and laundered the same to Dubai, South Africa and Singapore. The scam involved Madan Mitra, transport and sports minister under Mamta Banerjee's Trinamool Congress (TMC) government, Kunal Ghosh and Srijoy Bose, two TMC MPs, and Rajat Majumdar, another TMC leader. Union home secretary, Anil Goswami had to resign in February 2015 for admitting that he had called up CBI officers to dissuade them from calling Matang Sinha, former Union minister of UPA government, for questioning.

In 1997, Rose Valley Resorts & Plantation raised public funds to invest in rose plantation. It soon raised rupees 17,000 crore from public against booking of plots. Its boss Gautam Kundu was booked by ED under Prevention of Money Laundering Act. So far 2,300 accounts held by 27 companies with 30 banks have been frozen and property worth rupees 300 crore has been attached. TMC MP Sudip Bandopadhyaya was arrested by CBI in January 2017. Mamta Banerjee has alleged both Rose Valley and Saradha scams as politically motivated vendetta by BJP-led Centre and is one of the causes of bitter rift between her and NDA government, even though both were first exposed by UPA government. An estimated 18 lakh families lost their life-time savings in these ponzi scandals.

'VYAPAM', that stands for *Vyavsayik Pariksha Mandal,* is a scam in Madhya Pradesh that relates to forgery, rigging and impersonation in selection for government jobs for doctors, teachers, constables etc. Set up in 1970 to conduct entrance tests for MBBS course, it started conducting tests for professional courses and also for recruitment to various posts. Modus operandi of the scam was to let a qualified person appear on behalf of the favoured candidate, provide facility to the favoured candidates for copying in the exam or provide blank answer sheet to the favoured candidate after the exam to mark right answers. Hundreds of students were booked for fraud and rusticated from colleges for using unfair means. Allegations have been leveled against chief minister Shivraj Singh Chouhan and 30 others close to him. FIR against Governor Ram Naresh Yadav was quashed by the high court as he enjoyed constitutional immunity from prosecution. His son was also an accused and was found dead in March 2015. Witnesses and those probing details of the scam have been ruthlessly eliminated and so far over 50 deaths that occurred in road accidents, suicides, immolations, and similar other mysterious circumstances involved in this politically sensitive case have been reported. More than 2,000 suspects have been arrested, including former minister Laxmikant Sharma. Many political figures from Congress and BJP, and bureaucrats received large sums of money from educational institutions.

In a judgment in February 2017, Supreme Court cancelled degrees of 634 doctors saying that admissions obtained through a mass fraud cannot be condoned. We have to "build a nation on the touchstone of ethics and character" and to build a nation where only rule of law prevails. 'Sale' of MBBS and postgraduate seats in medical colleges is another scam that rakes in more than rupees 10,000 crore a year. This is all done in the garb of management and NRI quota and quota in minority institutions.

'Satyam' is India's biggest corporate accounting fraud. Ramalinga Raju, along with his brother B Rama Raju and brother-in-law DVS Raju set up Satyam Computer Services Ltd in Hyderabad in 1987. In 2006 he announced that the company's revenues crossed $ 1 billion but in January 2009 fraud of rupees 7,000 crore was disclosed in balance sheets. The economic offence having "deep-rooted conspiracy" caused a loss of rupees 14,000 crore to investors and unlawful gain of rupees 1,900 crore to Rajus and others. They were sentenced to 7-year jail and fine of rupees 5 crore each.

For providing residential accommodation to retired army personnel and war widows who lost their spouses during 1999 Kargil war, a posh 31-storey building was constructed by Adarsh Co-operative Housing Society on a prime estate in Kolaba, Mumbai. It is a sensitive coastal area in the vicinity of various defence establishments and mandatory Coastal Regulation Zone clearance had not been taken from the union environment ministry. Several politicians, bureaucrats, and military officials started flouting rules and got themselves the apartments allotted at below-market price. The owners included Chief of Naval Staff Madhavendra Singh, General NC Vij and General Deepak Kapoor, two chiefs of army staff, Chief Secretary and Collectors, family members of Ashok Chavan, former railway minister Suresh Prabhu and other politicians from NCP, Congress and BJP etc. Justice JA Patil Commission concluded in 2013 that 25 illegal allotments out of 102 were made including 22 purchases made by proxy. The report also inducted four former chief ministers of Maharashtra, Ashok Chavan, Vilaseao Deshmukh, Sushilkumar Shinde and Shivajirao Nilangekar Patil, two former urban development ministers and 12 top bureaucrats for various illegal acts. The report forced chief minister Ashok Chavan to resign. On a court decision 8 arrests were made which included two retired Major Generals, a retired Brigadier, a finance secretary and two IAS officers.

In April, 2016 Bombay High Court ordered demolition of the whole building for violation of norms. Exploring alternative possibilities to ensure that genuine flat owners are not hurt should have been explored. The building may be demolished but we may never see the demolition of the big fish and this scandal, like all others, may soon become history.

Several serving and former chief ministers and members of parliament have been sentenced for corruption charges. OP Chautala, former CM of Haryana, his son Ajay Chautala, his former political adviser, two IAS officers, besides 50 other accused were charged for taking bribe for recruiting 3,000 teachers and sentenced to 10 years in jail. In an 18-year old case of amassing illegal properties worth rupees 66.65 crore disproportionate to her known sources of income, Tamil Nadu chief minister, J Jayalalithaa, became the first CM in office to be convicted and was sentenced to 4-year jail term and fine of rupees 100 crore in September 2014. Other former CMs who have been jailed for graft are Lalu Prasad, Madhu Koda, BS Yeddyurappa and Jagannath Mishra. Virbhadra Singh, former Union minister is the third minister in UPA-2 to quit the Cabinet following corruption charges after A Raja and Dayanidhi Maran. The government is tightening the noose around the neck of the corrupt politicians but a lot more needs to be done. In all such scams and corruption cases courts are the saviour of democracy and nothing happens without their intervention.

Scams during UPA regime were not only confined to government and business sectors but had also polluted the gentleman's game of cricket and shamed the nation. Indian Premier League (IPL), world's richest cricket league currently valued at USD 4 billion, is a prominent source of many scams and scandals. Towels and hand signals are the simple instruments to turn the fate of this 'game of glorious uncertainties'. In July 2015, Supreme Court appointed a committee under Justice RM Lodha, former chief justice of India, who as a serving judge famously called the CBI a "caged parrot speaking in its master's voice" and cancelled all coal block allocations, suspended for two years two IPL teams for bringing "disrepute" and acting "contrary to the spirit of the game". Lalit Modi, first Chairman and Commissioner of IPL, charged for alleged financial irregularities and FEMA violations amounting to rupees 425 crore, is also alleged to have transferred millions of rupees to a company owned by Vasundra Raje, chief minister of Rajasthan and her son. This is termed as 'Modigate' and opposition parties accuse BJP of shielding Lalit Modi who has been in London since 2010. Financial irregularities have also been alleged in Delhi & District Cricket Association (DDCA) by BJP MP Kirti Azad. Prime Minister Manmohan Singh was blamed for twisting norms in 2004 and appointing Suresh Kalmadi, former Congress MP and President Indian

Olympic Association, as Chairman Commonwealth Games Organising Committee.

Leading politicians are hand-and-glove with cricket administration. Racket of spot-fixing is being traced to underworld don Dawood Ibrahim and the money is suspected to be channeled into terrorism and Bollywood. The guilty need to be severely punished and government must bring Board of Control for Cricket in India (BCCI), world's richest cricket body, under RTI.

Scams and scandals of corruption have not been confined to ministers and high bureaucrats but have also percolated to the lowest rung of administration in the ministries. In February 2015, 'Leakgate' episode rocked the government where peons and other officials were involved in pilferage of highly classified documents belonging to petroleum, coal and power ministries. Those arrested were selling documents for as low as rupees 5,000 which were subsequently supplied to business houses for lakhs of rupees giving them a windfall gain by making them aware of policy decisions earlier.

Besides the above famous scams, there have been many more like Cash-for-votes (2008) when BJP MPs said that they were paid to vote for US nuclear deal; CWG (2010) for irregularities in awarding contracts estimated at rupees 70,000 crore; Shashi Tharoor to help his wife Sunanda Pushkar in getting stake in Kochi IPL team; rupees 10 crore 'Railgate' in which railway minister, Pawan Kumar Bansal and his nephew were involved; railway bribery

(2013) when Pawan Kumar Bansal's nephew was caught with rupees 90 lakh bribe for a top railway job and the minister was made to resign; 'Scorpene' for allegation of kickbacks in rupees 16,000 crore for submarine deal; Tatra truck scam (2012) when army chief VK Singh alleged that he was offered a bribe to clear purchase of 1,676 trucks; Jaganmohan Reddy, son of YS Rajasekhara Reddy, chief minister of Andhra Pradesh for receiving over rupees 900 crore as bribe and rupees 3,000 crore allegedly paid to him by various cement companies for mining leases, besides 'chikki' in Maharashtra. Salman Khurshid, former union law minister, was accused of "misappropriating government funds" in a family trust and former BJP president, Nitin Gadkari for favouring a contractor in an irrigation project. Many more scams are certain to emerge, regardless of which party rules Centre and state capitals.

In cases involving individuals, Sahara India Pariwar's chief, Subrata Roy, was arrested for not refunding investor's money. Vijay Mallya has fled away after defrauding banks with crores of rupees. Nirav Modi, a diamond merchant, left the country after swindling thousands of crores of rupees from banks. The list is endless. Good governance is the key to stem the rot of corruption but government and opposition throw mud on each other and invariably try to evade responsibility.

Governments are not only responsible for keeping their eyes closed on various scams and scandals but also for shameful acts resulting in the loss of thousands of innocents lives. Bhopal gas tragedy is one of them. On the night of December 2, 1984, workers at Union Carbide fertilizer plant at Bhopal reported burning in eyes and suffocation due to gas leaking from a pressurised tank containing methyl isocyanate (MIC). Hundreds of people sleeping in shanties died, thousands died eventually, and over the next three decades more than 5 lakh suffered gas-leak related health issues, including lung cancer, and kidney and liver failure.

Warren Anderson, Chairman of Union Carbide was arrested on 7th December on his arrival in Bhopal. Bail was granted within 6 hours. He was flown to Delhi in a flight authorised by the then chief minister, Arjun Singh. Anderson went back to US the same day, never to return again and face trial. In fact, Congress government was responsible for his return to US under a settlement when Union Carbide paid a paltry amount of $470 million to the government in 1989. Justice for the victims was buried forever with Anderson's death in Florida at the age of 92. The incident is an ample testimony to the fact that in a weak democracy like India, it is easy to buy justice at the cost of thousands of lives of the poor. In scams or lives it is finally the democracy that suffers, sometimes mildly, sometimes beyond repair.

Corruption is the destructive enemy of democracy. It is a termite that weakens and consumes the edifice of democracy from within with no visible danger till it suddenly crumbles to pieces forever. The path of democracy paved with some loose gravel by Narasimha Rao and Atal Bihari Vajpayee was dismantled by the heavy load of corruption laden vehicles during the two tenures of UPA and suffered irreparable damage.

9

ON SLIPPERY SLOPE

Paradoxically, greed, that is programmed into our genes and has helped in human evolution and progress, is also responsible for his downward slide. The instinct of greed gives birth to the menace of corruption and is the genesis of political corruption that weakens the foundations of democracy. With all the laudable inventions of science, no medicine has so far been invented for the eradication of this human virus.

Immoral acquisition of wealth destroys the energy and enthusiasm of people believing in honesty and there should be zero tolerance towards any kind of corruption. Outrage against corruption is fast gaining strength but lack of conviction against illegal amassing of wealth has gravely eroded public faith in the political and social systems. Supreme Court also observed that corruption has become national economic terror and is eating away the fundamental core of elective democracy and constitutional governance. It is the biggest obstacle to economic development.

Land grabbing has been a significant source of political corruption in connivance with the government and corrupt bureaucracy. 'Public purpose' in the earlier law to acquire land for infrastructure, institutions and industries always exploited the poor farmers to acquire their precious fertile agricultural land only to transfer it to realtors for personal gain. The new Land Acquisition Act enacted by Parliament in 2013, stipulates to provide just and fair compensation and rehabilitation of those whose land is taken away for constructing roads, buildings or factories. The law also stipulates mandatory consent of at least 70% of affected people for acquiring land for public-private partnership projects (PPP) and 80% for acquiring land for private companies. 'Public purpose' has been clearly defined and the new law is farmer-friendly. The land cannot be vacated until the entire compensation is awarded to the affected parties besides review of a report by Social Impact Assessment (SIA).

Business and industrial houses, however, fear that new legislation will make land acquisition for them more difficult and will adversely affect business. Even small projects may take years to acquire land and environmental clearance logjams may put them at disadvantage against the competitive nations.

One glaring example of political corruption is of land grabbing during UPA by Robert Vadra, son-in-law of Congress president, Sonia Gandhi. Vadra's Skylight Hospitality bought 3.53 acres of land in Gurgaon

(Haryana) for rupees 7.5 crore. He got permission from the town and country planning department within 18 days to build a commercial colony there. Over the next few months, Vadra transferred the land and permission to DLF for rupees 58 crore, a windfall gain. On the report of Justice SN Dhingra Commission, FIRs were filed against Vadra and, Bhupinder Singh Hooda, former chief minister of Haryana and the case is pending in the court.

'Roshni' is another land scam which involved the alleged encroachment of 2,50,000 acres of J & K state land by the powerful land mafia in league with politicians, revenue and police officers. It is named after the J & K State Land (Vesting of Ownership to the Occupants) Act, 2001, popularly called the Roshni Act. The government aimed to earn rupees 25,000 crore but CAG pointed out that only rupees 76 crore had been earned. The law was repealed in 2018 when the state came under Governor's rule.

Congress alone is not the only party under scanner on corruption for land grabbing. There are countless cases involving politicians across all political parties that are a great menace to the growth of democracy. Vohra Committee in its report observed, "There has been a rapid spread and growth of criminal gangs, armed *senas*, drug mafias, smuggling gangs, drug peddlers and economic lobbies in the country which have, over the years, developed an extensive network of contacts with the bureaucrats/government functionaries at local levels, media persons and strategically located individuals in the non-state sectors."

Like land grabbing, sand mining is another source of political corruption. It is a lucrative business which destroys the riverain environment and has deplorable impact on river ecologies. There is a blatant nexus between the political leaders, sand mafia and the builders for digging and mining contracts given to political heavy weights or to their near ones. Stringent rules curbing mining from river beds on environmental grounds has created huge shortage of sand, making people more dependent on sand mafia for supplies. Mining of minor minerals, like boulders, gravel, ordinary sand, lime shell, *kankar* etc. falls under the power of the state and responsibility for framing rules and their promulgation rests on the state governments. Many honest police officers have been killed by the mafia and crushed under the wheels of the dumpers.

The monster of corruption can't be killed in a week. Its roots have to be constantly attacked. It needs systematic reforms and genuine political intent to eradicate it. The honest must be given moral strength through political and legal protection and the crooked and the business-politics-nexus must be ruthlessly slaughtered. Nothing emboldens the corrupt more than the belief that there will be no or negligible consequences for any corrupt behaviour. The scope of corruption is also directly proportional to the number of authorities wielding power to stop it.

Corruption exists not only in our social life but has also become an integral part of our political system. Out of the numerous sources, dubious funding of political parties in elections is the fountain-head of political corruption and a great threat to the health and survival of democracy. About 88% of the total income of political parties is through grants, donations, sale of coupons, contributions that include voluntary donations below rupees 20,000, and collections through other shady sources. Due to loopholes in 'The Representation of the People Act' and lack of transparency and accountability, details of these sources are generally kept as a close secret and are not available in public domain.

Income of four national parties – BJP, CPM, NCP, BSP – increased from rupees 920 crore in 2013-2014 to rupees 1,275 crore in 2014-2015. BJP and Congress together account for more than 80% of total funds collected by all parties from all sources. It is shocking that Congress declared that for the years 2009-11 only 14% of its income was from donations and rest was from a mysterious category called "sale of coupons". Bahujan Samaj Party (BSP) kept the law in dark about the identity of its donors. BJP declared that its major income was from an unexplained entity called *Aajiwan Sahayog Nidhi*. Central Information Commission (CIC) gave a landmark decision on June 3, 2013 that political parties will be liable to reveal the identities of all those donors so far dubiously concealed.

Democracy exists in the country but is awfully absent in the life and working of political parties and they do not quite share their transparency in political finances. India is one of 10% countries in the world that allow political parties or candidates to receive unidentified donations. Here a party can receive an anonymous amount up to rupees 20,000 and the donor can avoid the legal obligation to be identified by donating multiple sums amounting to less than this amount. According to figures compiled by the Association for Democratic Reforms, an NGO working for probity in elections, in the eleven years between 2004-15, parties got contributions worth rupees 6800 crore from unknown sources, with total income of rupees 11,367 crore. Congress made around rupees 4000 crore from unknown donors while BJP followed close with rupees 3273 crore. Samajwadi Party collected 94% out of its total income of rupees 819 crore from unknown sources. BSP which collected rupees 764 crore, did not declare even a single donor, as all its contributions were less than rupees 20,000. Aam Aadmi Party (AAP), formed in 2013 on the plank of eliminating corruption from elections and ensuring transparency in political funding, had 57% of its income out of total of rupees 110 crore from unknown sources. For its Delhi elections in February 2015 the party received rupees 11.4 crore in donations in one month before elections. Four companies donated a combined rupees 2 crore to AAP, just a few days before the polls when they had no regular business, no profits in their balance sheets and no proper business address. India needs a credible election finance regime with real teeth to check under-the-table funding.

Big business houses contribute huge sums, often to several parties, through cash. Cash donations to political parties should be banned and transfer of finances should be through banking channels only to ensure transparency both of the parties and the corporate houses. It is estimated that only 1% of this contribution is utilised for political activities and rest is simply pocketed. Candidates and parties are required to declare their income to the IT department but most have been evasive about 80% of their income in their annual returns before the IT department and the Election Commission. NDA government passed a legislation making corporate and individual contributions to a political party fully tax deductible. It also made it compulsory for parties to submit to the Election Commission a list of donations of rupees 20,000 and above. While these measures introduced some accountability to election financing, there are far too many escape routes for parties.

Election expenditure is another grey area and expenses on elections are brazenly flouted. Cost of elections has risen exponentially and ceiling on election expenditure is unpractical and abysmally low. According to revised limits, a candidate cannot spend more than rupees 40 lakh in a parliamentary constituency and not more than rupees 16 lakh for an assembly constituency. This is besides the free airtime on state-owned television and radio networks allocated in 1998. With the revised limits a candidate cannot send even a post card to 20 lakh voters in a constituency. Most of them violate it and spend between rupees 5 and 10 crore. Mounting costs of election campaigns result in candidates taking recourse to incomplete and inaccurate expense statements and under-reporting their expenditure.

The government must initiate electoral reforms and make all political parties accountable for their income and expenditure to check corruption in political financing. Audited accounts of all political parties, certified by the Election Commission, must be available online for the public. Political parties are required to file their election expenditure within 75 days of assembly elections and within 90 days of Lok Sabha polls failing which their recognition can be withdrawn by the Election Commission. In 1996, Supreme Court in the Common Cause Judgment ordered all political parties to file income tax returns. Even then many parties fail to do so or do it after the time limit.

The link between black money and political funding had been noted by both the Santhanam Committee (1964) and the Wanchoo Committee (1971). Nearly 40 years ago, Supreme Court also said, "Money power casts a sinister shadow on our elections...The likely evasion of law by using big money through political parties is a source of pollution of the Indian political process."

Violation of model code of conduct is another ploy for political corruption. Poll officials and flying squads are ever vigilant to keep a hawk eye to check politicians from violating it but almost all candidates find creative ways to circumvent the law. In a classic case in rural Orissa, politicians organised fake wedding receptions, complete with 'bride', 'groom, *pundit* and 'parents' of the 'couple'. Promise of free bottle of liquor for each male guest, a *saree* for each woman guest, and a lavish wedding feast for everyone lured the villagers. There is no dearth of such crafty devices in the fertile Indian minds.

All political parties make corruption a matter of national concern in their election campaign but unfortunately are 'soft' on corruption in their own den. Corruption is reported to be highest in political parties at 86%, followed by police at 75% and lowest in military at 20%. All politicians are not corrupt. Aberration exists in all walks of life and presumption of endemic greed, corruption or collusion is flawed.

Money and muscle-power are at the root of all political and electoral corruption. Political parties in fact run powerful 'parallel government' in connivance with mafia, corrupt bureaucrats and local goons. All parties are victim of this virus and are not interested in cleaning their stables. With all their ideological and political differences, corruption-ridden politicians from all parties united to amend the RTI Act in order to exclude political parties from its ambit. They may be rivals but they are wedded to safeguard their personal interests at the cost of national interest. "All thieves are cousins", goes the common rural saying. Governments are also formed by corrupt political parties that behave like a Parliamentary dictatorship and not like a Parliamentary democracy. Political corruption will continue to rampantly grow unless political parties are brought under RTI.

Free, fair and effective democracy costs money and parties need huge resources to sustain them. Limit on election expenditure has to be raised and one way is to allow open contributions by the people to individual candidates through bank account. Dinesh Goswammi Committee and Indrarjit Gupta Committee recommended partial state funding of elections and establishment of a separate election fund. For transparency, cap on poll expenses may be abolished and instead there may be mandatory auditing of party accounts. On the issue of state funding, APJ Abdul Kalam said, "State has to fund the election expenses of the candidates, and the accounts should be scrutinised by the Election Commission." At rupees 100 a vote, total state funding would come to rupees 4,200 crore which may become 10,000 crores due to bye-polls and mid-term elections. Compare it to farm loans waiver of rupees 60,000 crore in 2008, subsidies of rupees 44,000 crore for petroleum, rupees 75,000 crore for food and rupees 33,000 crore for MGNREGA. This amount of election funding is a small price for transparency and will restore the dignity of democracy. A national election fund can be created to which corporate bodies may contribute and a formula for distribution can be worked out. Many countries of Europe, Asia and parts of America have successfully implemented it. The idea needs to be explored further as a permanent solution to reduce corruption in election financing.

Community can play a significant role in checking corruption. In a democracy, we need a massive social movement to raise collective voice against the corrupt and elect honest representatives. Public pressure through different platforms is perhaps the only way to bring about reforms as political parties have no incentive to change. Besides public pressure, strict and enforceable anti-corruption laws are essential as prosecution alone cannot reform a faulty system.

Shadow economy, as parallel black-money economy is called, is another significant source of corruption. It is broadly defined as the income derived from economic activities that circumvent the government's regulation and taxation. In fact, all unreported incomes form 'black economy' and 'black money' is its tiny component. There are innumerable organised and unorganised systems for the generation of black money in India and the most significant are corruption in awarding contracts, over-invoicing and under-invoicing in business, gold retail, and cash transfers in real estate sector. Shadow economy in India is 22.2% of its GDP and is aided and supported by a weak institutional mechanism and socio-cultural behaviour.

It is estimated that more than 50% of India's economy is black. About half of this is consumed while the remaining half is saved. Of the savings about 20% is taken out of the country. In a study of 135 countries in 2017 by Global Financial Integrity (GFI), India had the third-highest trade related illicit financial flow with USD 83.5 billion (rupees 5.8 lakh crore) escaping the government's tax net. This is the most damaging economic problem plaguing Indian economy and depriving it of the much-needed capital for basic amenities and services.

Tracing illegal outflow of black money is very complex. It is estimated that black money deposited by Indians in Swiss banks has increased by 286% during 2019-20 and now stands at rupees 20,700 crore. Besides taxes not paid on this enormous sum, it may be put to use for various criminal activities or may come back to India through various methods such as *hawala*, mispricing, FDI etc. The International Consortium of Investigative Journalists (ICIJ) published 'Panama Papers' exposing the names of renowned world personalities and heads of governments who have hidden their incomes abroad. It had 500 names of Indians and after further investigations the government submitted 627 names to the SC in October, 2014. Things have remained the same and it looks like a wild goose chase. Like black holes it swallows up everything and is apparently impervious to scrutiny.

Sustained efforts are needed to catalyse far-reaching reforms in global financial and tax systems and must separate wheat from chaff and distinguish between "black money" and "blood money".

The problem of black money in India is structural and going after the foreign component of black money is just a diversion. A government commissioned study in 2013 reportedly calculated the size of black economy to be as high as 70% of GDP bulk of which is right here in the country. India needs strong measures to rationalise the tax structure, initiate greater reforms in vulnerable sectors like gold retail and real estate, and move towards a cashless economy. BJP government delivered a stunning surprise by scrapping 500 and 1,000 rupee notes from the midnight of November 8, 2016 but the result of this scraping has not been very encouraging and productive due to poor implementation. In January 1978, Morarji Desai-led Janta Government had demonetised 500, 1,000 and 10,000 rupee notes to curb black money.

Since 1948, about 40 commissions have looked at the problem of black money with zero result. There is a tirade of vested interests of politicians and complete absence of political will to tackle the problem. The government should crack down on those tax payers who attempt to conceal assets and income subject to Indian laws. Severe punitive action should be taken against income generated from illegal activities like drug running, arms dealing, real estate, *hawala* transactions etc. More important battle against black money has to be waged at home so that unaccounted money cannot be transferred abroad.

Besides corruption in our political and social systems, criminalisation of politics is the very negation of democratic values that has tarnished the name of Indian democracy. A study conducted in 2016 by the Association for Democratic Reforms (ADR), a Delhi-based think tank, analysed that of the 62,847 parliament and assembly candidates since 2004, 18% had criminal cases against them and 8% had declared 'serious' criminal cases. The study revealed that out of 620 ministers of 29 states and 2 UTs, 210 (34%) had declared criminal cases against themselves out of which 113 ministers had declared serious criminal cases. The situation at the centre was equally pathetic. Out of 78 Union Council of Ministers analysed, 24 (31%) had declared criminal cases against themselves related to murder, kidnapping and crimes against women. In this connection the Supreme Court observed that the ethos of the Constitution expected the PM and CMs not to include a person in their council of ministers if a trial court has framed charges against him. It said, "constitutional morality" requires that those in "conflict with law and involved in offences of moral turpitude should not be allowed to discharge duty as ministers… Rest is to be left to the wisdom of the PM."

An analysis of over 60,000 records of candidates and winners since 2004 shows that while only 12% 'clean' candidates without any taint win, around 23% of tainted candidates win, making a mockery of our democracy. Since crime plays a greater role in this messy competitive election scenario, all political parties are tempted to field tainted candidates. In 2018 the government informed the Supreme Court that 1765 (36%) MPs and MLAs were facing criminal trial in 3045 cases.

Wealth of MPs and MLAs facing criminal cases rose to rupees 4.30 crore on an average and those facing serious charges, like murder, kidnapping and rape were on top of the heap with average assets of rupees 4.38 crore. The study also revealed that for 1,615 of the 4,181 candidates the assets increased by 200%, for 684 by 500% and for 317 by over 1,000%. Average assets of all legislators grew ten times in five-year term. Average assets of 165 MPs re-elected to the 16th Lok Sabha shot up a whopping 137% between 2009 and 2014.

It is often argued that criminalisation of politics merely reflects criminalisation of society. But the figures show that whereas one in every 30 MPs elected in the 2009 general elections faced murder or related charges, only one in 1,061 of the same age group faced the same in the populace at large. Same is the position in other crimes.

Politicians with criminal background thrive because they have "currency" and have 22% chance of winning as against 7% chance with non-criminal background. The data also showed that the poorest 20% of candidates, in terms of personal financial assets, had 1% chance of winning Parliamentary elections while the richest quintile had greater than 25% chance. Today money and power add to the probability of victory, and morality and ideology are only camouflage for criminality to garner votes and come to power. Former US Vice-president Al Gore remarked, "Incestuous coupling of wealth and power posed the deadliest threat to democracy."

In re-contesting elections also, candidates with money and criminal background have higher chance of and better record of winning. Political parties gave tickets second time to 74% of candidates accused of heinous crimes despite being aware of their dubious background. Wealth of re-contesting candidates has grown to 134% in less than five years. The myth that money and muscle power win polls only in backward states is also wrong. In Delhi, out of 68 legislators, 29 had criminal cases pending against them, of which six faced serious charges like rape and murder. Delhi has also the highest number of *crorepati* MLAs.

Growth of number of political parties has also encouraged criminalisation of politics. In 1950 there were only 54 political parties and today we have six recognised National Parties and several hundred regional parties. Most of the developed countries have at most half a dozen. From late 1970s the criminals began to be used freely by political parties to intimidate voters, capture booths, stuff ballot boxes etc. In 1990s these miscreants realised that instead of working for candidates they could reap greater benefits by themselves becoming candidates and forming their own political parties.

It is difficult to say why voters would prefer a wealthy "tainted" candidate to "clean" alternative. Perhaps this ensures their physical safety, access to government benefits and social insurance. It may also be due to our centuries of slavish mentality of seeking shelter under the powerful. It is normally said that four Indians cannot move together unless they have the fifth to drive them. Onus for liberating democracy from criminalisation rests only and only on voter. US President Franklin Roosevelt also said, "Democracy cannot succeed unless those who express their choice are prepared to choose wisely. The real safeguard of democracy, therefore, is education."

In a landmark judgment in 2002 the Supreme Court remarked, "To maintain the purity of elections and to bring transparency in the process of election, the Election Commission can ask the candidates about the expenditure incurred by the political parties and this transparency would include transparency of a candidate who seeks election or re-election." To weaken the apex court ruling the government passed a legislation saying that only those who get elected were required to declare their assets and criminal antecedents and not every candidate. This was quashed by the court in 2003 but all political parties met and unanimously resolved to nullify the SC judgment.

Pushing for electoral reforms, the SC directed political parties to publish in a local and a national newspaper the entire criminal history of their candidates for assembly and Lok Sabha elections with reasons that prompted them to field suspected candidates. In another historic judgment on July 10, 2013, Supreme Court struck down a section of the Section 8(4) of 'The Representation of the People Act', 1951, and held that "Sitting Members of Parliament and state legislators… convicted for an offence carrying a sentence of two years and more will immediately be unseated. Those in jail or in police custody cannot contest elections or cast vote to legislative bodies though it would not apply to those subjected to preventive detention under any law." Unable to swallow the bitter pill, the government again tried to take the ordinance route. Rahul Gandhi, then Congress Vice-president, trashed the ordinance as "complete nonsense". Ordinance was withdrawn and the Bill was buried.

Unfortunately, our MPs and MLAs never use their unanimity for any good cause. All political parties unite when it hurts their self-interest and then they become petitioner, respondent and judge. There are no conscience keepers in the parties to support genuine democratic reforms. Political parties fling charges about corruption but have no serious impulse to clean up the system. Morality and integrity are virtues that come from within and no law can force them from outside. The credibility of our politicians is lowest in recent years and this has dealt a destructive blow to the smooth working of democracy. Democracy can be strengthened by adopting and promoting democratic values and shunning criminal tendencies.

Judiciary is a beacon of hope for cleansing criminal malcontents from Indian political system. Lot has been done to check this menace but it will take significantly more sweeping measures to root out crime-politics nexus. Trimming branches will not help, roots need to be attacked.

Lokpal is another hope for minimising corruption from our political system. It is an anti-corruption ombudsman, concept of which was borrowed from Sweden. The term 'Lokpal' is derived from Sanskrit and means "Caretaker of People". The Act "seeks to provide for the establishment of the institution of Lokpal to inquire into allegations of corruption against certain public functionaries for matters connecting them." In India it was the result of India Against Corruption movement in 2011 led by Anna Hazare.

Lokpal and Lokayukt Act, commonly known as Lokpal Act, came into force from 16 January 2014. It can inquire into any allegation of corruption against PM, ministers, MPs and Group A or B officers of the central government who become corrupt in the hands of unscrupulous politicians. Similarly, Lokayuktas will be formed in each state. Formation of Lokpal and Lokayuktas, as a pro-people legislation, is key to the success of an anti-corruption drive. Though a good beginning, it has no magic wand that will banish corruption overnight. It has some glaring omissions as well. There is no mention in it of the Citizens' Charter and does not lay down specific delivery timelines to redress complaints against government authorities and fix responsibility for non-delivery of the same. Without it Lokpal is like a "tiger wearing dentures and can run into a stampede." Protection of whistleblowers who make public interest disclosures against corruption has been completely missed. Again, the Act keeps judiciary well out of its reach which makes it toothless. With all the criticism, Lokpal will break the nexus between criminals, politicians and bureaucrats, and weed out corruption at higher level to a great extent. Lower bureaucracy, however, continues to be relatively more corrupt, has strong unions and holds the administration to ransom by holding files and facts to disrupt work.

Across all liberal democracies, the basic principle of rule of law and accountability apply to all law enforcement agencies. India must follow suit with structural reforms that ensure this end. Enforcing rule of law and transparency in political system are the cardinal principles of democracy absence of which throttles democracy and puts its very existence in peril. Lack of transparency and absence of accountability are great facilitators of corruption. Robert Klitgaard, a world- famous authority on corruption, mathematically formulated, $C=M+D-A$ where C stands for corruption, M for monopoly, D for discretion and A for accountability. So, corruption can be minimised by reducing monopoly and discretion, and improving accountability. Woodrow Wilson, former US President said, "Government ought to be all outside and no inside." Similarly, William Gladstone remarked, "It is the duty of the government to make it difficult for the people to do wrong, easy to do right."

There is no magic solution that will eliminate corruption altogether. It may not be completely eradicated but can certainly be minimised to a large extent by reducing excessive regulations, reforming licencing system, minimising discretionary powers of bureaucracy, and making laws more transparent. Lack of political will is the single most significant obstacle in its eradication.

Real progress against corruption requires preventive and educational reforms that drive social change. There are no permanent solutions in life but waiting for 100% success merely ensures 0% success. Alan Greenspan said, "Corruption, embezzlement, fraud, exist everywhere. What successful economies do is keep it to a minimum." Though corruption is a universal phenomenon, in India it has rampantly grown due to our socio-cultural character. Democracy in India is under constant threat and will continue to struggle unless strong measures are taken to weed out corruption from our social and political systems.

10

JUNGLE TRAIL

Democracy in India has been struggling during its journey of last seven decades. Besides numerous socio-economic reasons, steady decline in our parliamentary system has been very significant. The centre of gravity in any democracy is best measured by the credibility of its Parliament, the sacred temple of democracy. Unfortunately, Indian Parliament has often been a scene of inaction and misdemeanor. Atal Bihari Vajpayee, one of the most charismatic parliamentarians, stressed that Parliament is a place "where hopes, aspirations and frustrations of people of this country should be reflected and echoed."

Primarily, Parliament is a forum to deliberate, debate and legislate. Legislative decision-making needs to be more participatory but policy discourse and debate are woefully inadequate in Indian Parliament. There was a time when debates in Parliament were of very high caliber, with the right mix of oratory, substance, decorum and wit. In the first two decades of Independence, politicians refrained from casting aspersions on the character of their opponents in the Parliament. During and after Indira years, political debates deteriorated, became increasingly personalised and lung power overwhelmed elegance and substance of argument. Today, the sorry spectacle is that under the very nose of the Speaker, members increasingly intrude into the well, carrying placards and shouting slogans. Fisticuffs, pepper spray, shards of glass, throwing chairs and water bottles, slippers zooming, uprooting and hurling microphones as missiles, tearing copies of Bills, frequent walkouts, shouting down at rivals, and brawls turn the Parliament into a wrestling ground and battlefield. Name calling, below-the-belt attacks, sickeningly unparliamentary language and exchange of abuses unbecoming of an elected representative have also become more frequent to settle personal and political scores. Sadly, Parliament fiddles while India burns.

In 1997, Rajya Sabha had drawn up a code of conduct that "Members must not do anything that brings disrepute to Parliament and affects their credibility." Surprisingly, Lok Sabha has not adopted any code of conduct for its members. Indiscriminate disruptions have no penalties, though Speaker Lok Sabha and Chairman Rajya Sabha are both invested with wide-ranging disciplinary powers to suspend or expel errant members. Irish MPs in Britain used to be physically picked up by marshals and thrown out on the street. Our Parliament is becoming more undemocratic these days and this is further compounded by frequent disruptions since the members enjoy immunity before law in their acts in the Parliament.

Parliament has to broaden the definition of "disrepute" to the House and frame a strict code of conduct for the members and then follow it rigourously. Responsibility for bringing disrepute to the Parliament rests completely with our elected representatives. Stricter punishment for unruly behaviour is imperative as worse will come and democratic system will collapse if counter-measures are not urgently implemented.

State assemblies are not free from similar rowdy scenes. In March 2015 in Kerala assembly, opposition members stormed the speaker's dais, overturned his chair, damaged furniture and engaged themselves in violent scuffle that left nine MLAs and 12 watch-and-ward staff injured. A Congress MLA was bitten by a lady MLA. Another classic example is of a chief minister tearing the Agricultural Reforms Act that had already been adopted by the state assembly. Such shameful episodes leave Indian democracy in tears.

Globally, our Parliament has become a laughing stock as we have made a mockery of our democratic system. Our democracy has matured in years but our political class has become more immature and is still struggling to understand the dynamics of parliamentary system. Parliamentary democracy demands that legislators do their homework and argue their case on the basis of facts and reason. Instead of debating the issue at hand, they sidetrack it mainly due to lack of adequate preparation, ignorance of facts and poor knowledge. Addressing the nation on the eve of Republic Day in 2015, President Pranab Mukherjee said, "Enacting laws without discussion impacts the law-making role of the Parliament...We need a Parliament that debates, discusses and decides." Not only in Parliament, debates on TV are also high on decibels but low on reason, facts and linguistic restraint. Earlier difference of opinion was taken with an open mind and without questioning bona fides. Today, rhetoric has overtaken substance thereby reducing public debate to the lowest common denominator of 'I am right', 'you are wrong'.

Due to disruptions and unhealthy debates, the Parliament has the abysmal record of passing bills. The first Lok Sabha in 1952 passed 333 bills and only 7 lapsed while the 15th passed 165 bills with 126 pending. So far as discussion time is concerned, 20 bills were passed with less than five minutes discussion. Same is the case with Rajya Sabha. It passed 5 bills in less than 5 minutes. Record of state assemblies is appalling. Between 2011-13 Haryana passed a whopping 56% bills without any discussion, 6% with less than 5 minutes of discussion and only 5% were discussed for more than 20 minutes. Adjournments have become a common feature of our Parliament. In its entire history, the British House of Commons hasn't been adjourned once. India can claim just the opposite. In India there isn't a single day when Parliament is not adjourned. Disruptions and adjournments are a severe blow to the institution of Parliament and tarnish the fair name of Indian democracy.

Disruptions not only delay legislation but also cost the nation time and money. One hour of Lok Sabha costs the exchequer rupees 1.5 crore and of Rajya Sabha rupees 1.1 crore. Total loss to the exchequer would be astronomical as the time lost in the last 25 years was more than 2,100 hours. Penalties ought to apply for politics of obstruction with no work leading to no pay.

There is no legal requirement for minimum sittings of Parliament or state assemblies, except that not more than six months should elapse between two successive sessions. Repeated recommendations seeking a minimum of 120 sittings a year for each legislature have been ignored. Lok Sabha sittings were 127 days yearly in 1950s but continued dipping since mid-1970 and fell to 71 for the 15th Lok Sabha with dubious distinction of complete washout sessions. While Indian Parliament meets on an average for 67 days in a year, Britain's meets for 150 days and US Congress for 200 days. State assemblies have no better record. During the decade, 2003-2013, Delhi assembly met only for an average of 5.7% of time per year, Goa 7.1%, Bihar 8.4%, and Haryana for a shocking 3.5%.

There is marked rise in disruptions not only within the Parliament but outside also. The propensity of various forms of agitations like *dharnas*, shutdowns and hunger-strikes are on the rise. Cynical violent mobs destroy national property and stone throwing has become a routine in such agitations. Political parties and other constitutional authorities are also not free from this menace. Chief minister of Delhi staged a *dharna* in order to get some policemen suspended forgetting that as a role model he is elected to provide good governance rather than hold system to ransom. For his demand of Delhi as a full-fledged state also there is no place for unconstitutional methods. Most capital cities around the world have special government mechanisms and different models are available in other national capitals to balance democratic and security exigencies. In June 2018, he went to meet the LG with an appointment and then refused to leave his office unless his demands were met. On flimsy issues and when required to appear in the courts even for serious corruption cases, there is massive show of strength by the party supporters, prominent leaders and even chief ministers with scant regard to the dignity of democratic norms. '*Satyagraha*' by Congress leaders on the appearance of Rahul Gandhi and Sonia Gandhi before ED in National Herald case is a significant example. Taking recourse to such unconstitutional methods runs counter to the spirit of parliamentary democracy and is a disgrace to the nation. They have no justification in a democracy and "are nothing but the grammar of anarchy and the sooner they are abandoned, the better for us", said Ambedkar.

Democratic disagreement is a common feature of a parliamentary democracy and must be voiced but not at the cost of dignity and honour of it. Reminding political parties on their responsibilities, Pranab Mukherjee said,

"It is incumbent on the ruling party and opposition to sit together and find a workable solution to avoid disruptions." He also said, "Majority has the mandate to rule while opposition has the right to oppose, expose, and if numbers permit, to depose…A noisy minority cannot be allowed to gag a patient majority." Indian Parliament has in fact become a federation of anarchists. Distinguished sociologist Andre Betelle says, "The chronic mistrust between government and opposition impairs the foundation of democracy."

Strong and active opposition is inevitable in a democracy since politics like nature cannot sustain vacuum. A productive parliamentary system depends on a constructive opposition. However, a responsible opposition must work towards a common and coordinated agenda, discover a political line of action that has resonance with the aspirations of the people and discover an acceptable rallying point. Unfortunately, we have today perennial deadlocks caused by inconsistent stands taken by political parties. Government proposes and Opposition opposes with nothing to propose. MPs have in effect created 'Right to Disrupt' and a rowdy and disruptive minority can today stifle even a majority government.

Opposing just for the sake of opposing and sacrificing important national issues is evident from two pertinent examples. Hold up of FDI in insurance and GST had nothing to do with ideology. Vajpayee-led NDA government wanted to raise FDI limit to foreign players in insurance sector in 1999 but Congress opposed it. When Congress-led UPA came to power in 2004, BJP created roadblock. In 2014, BJP government approved hike in foreign investment ceiling but now the Congress used every trick possible to delay it. Finally, the Parliament, with the support of Congress, raised FDI cap from 26% to 49% in March 2015 delaying a significant economic project for 16 years. Same story was repeated in case of GST Bill in 2016 conceived over 30 years back with BJP and Congress opposing it when in opposition and supporting it when in power. No party is free from the virus of mindless obstructionism. A vibrant and progressive democracy certainly needs an opposition but not a rag-tag brand that opposes everything sacrificing national interests disastrous to the smooth working of a successful democracy.

Aspirations of the electorate are rising and India's public opinion may not tolerate such a sorry state of affair for a long time. There is no self-correcting solution in the current situation. Still, it must come from within. The blame for this sordid state of affairs must be shared by all parties. With Parliament fading into the background and its dysfunction leading to policy paralysis, Supreme Court has become the epicenter of legislative activity. If Indian democracy is safe, it is because of the vigilance of its citizens and strength of unbending judiciary.

Emergence of irresponsible coalition-politics has further added to the decline of our democratic system. After independence, first was Nehruvian era with huge majorities in Parliament. This was followed by Indira Gandhi's authoritarian control of Congress subjugating inner-party democracy and stifling opposition. Rajiv Gandhi had a commanding majority in the Parliament but could not effectively deal with opposition. The present era of patchwork and experimental coalitions started after him. Party leaders have now come to realise that consensus can no longer flow from charismatic leadership or the power of brute parliamentary majorities and insatiable coalitions is the only option.

Coalition politics particularly requires vastly complex set of interpersonal skills of 'political management'. It requires mutual give-and-take and the ability to negotiate with ideological adversaries to find workable solutions and get around seemingly insurmountable obstacles and 'policy paralysis'. Diplomacy is an essential part of maneuvering the coalition partners in case of razor-thin majority keeping stubborn, greedy, corrupt and opportunistic partners at bay. In coalitions there is no political isolation and there is complete absence of political untouchability. Kinship here is no guarantee of peace and loyalty is a variable virtue. Coalition breeds strangest of bedfellows, with yesterday's sworn foes cosying up as faithful friends. Coalition slope is very slippery and greed only binds the partners together. Pranab Mukherjee rightly said, "A fractured government, hostage to whimsical opportunists, is always an unhappy eventuality."

Political coalitions need to shed their destructive tendencies and adopt constructive national goals and work as a reformist coalition. The government in power must also respect the sentiments of the coalition partners. In mythology Ravana remains the ultimate metaphor for coalition politics. His ten heads were barely on speaking terms with one another and were a symbol of disaster. Coalitions today are like his ten heads forming an unholy alliance with no clarity on the national policy vision which creates hurdles in the democratic path.

Indian democracy has to survive now with a vast set of diversities and increasing influence of regional parties. Coalitions have come to be known for inefficiency, sloth and corruption but are here to stay. Marriage and politics have much in common with one difference. Unlike in marriage, politics is a love-game where pre-or-post alliances involve the give-and-take not of dowry but of ministerial berths. Tragically, just as unholy matrimonial alliances end in dowry deaths, political marriages also suffer the same tragic fate, the victim being the bride called democracy.

To admirably serve the cause of greedy coalition politics and appeasement of disgruntled elements within the party, government resorts to multiplication of ministries. The first cabinet of independent India had around a dozen portfolios, which had gone up to 53 by

2015 and a whopping 66 in 2021. Government must check mindless multiplication of ministries and banish or amalgamate some with other ministry to trim down expenditure. It needs strong political will to implement all these reforms which the greedy coalitions woefully lack due to political and bureaucratic cowardice.

Cabinet or council of ministers is the core of parliamentary democracy and its erosion dents its spirit. British parliamentarian, Patrick Gordon Walker said, "basically Cabinet is a constitutional mechanism to ensure that before important decisions are reached, many sides of the question are weighed and considered." Conventional wisdom also tells that many minds are better than one. Nehru also said, "I take the advice of my colleagues in the Cabinet. That is the way of democratic government." During UPA rule and particularly UPA-2, there was a near-complete subversion of Cabinet system due to the dominance of Sonia Gandhi and timidity of the tame duck, Manmohan Singh. Sanjay Baru claims that Sonia Gandhi was privy to Cabinet files and used her political secretary Ahmed Patel and her loyalists in the prime minister's office and Cabinet to call the shots in appointments and interfere in the formulation and implementation of government policies. This resulted in each ministry running as per the whims and fancies of a regional or central strap leading to too many tails wagging the dog. Political scientist Pratap Bhanu Mehta also says, "The long and short of it is that the PM was humiliated."

Constitution under Article 123 provides for the provision of ordinance as urgent measure of legislation taken when the situation cannot wait for Parliament to convene and it has to be validated by the next legislative session, or else it lapses. Like erosion of Cabinet system, promulgation of ordinance also dents parliamentary democracy. Incessant ordinance is parliamentary retreat from its core function of lawmaking. Pranab Mukherjee said that ordinances are meant "to meet an extraordinary situation under extraordinary circumstances". Opposition calls the ordinance process as "Constitutional terrorism". So far 637 ordinances have been promulgated with maximum 195 by Indira Gandhi. No government is free from this menace.

Another misuse of the Constitutional process is the imposition of President Rule as provided in Article 356 of the Constitution. President's rule in a state can be imposed for one year, subject to approval of both Houses of Parliament within two months of the proclamation. This power was used by the centre 20 times from 1950-70, 63 times from 1970-90, 27 times from 1991-2010 and 5 times from 2011-16. Its use should be very rare and a government at the centre should refrain from using it for personal vendetta against a constitutionally elected government. Ambedkar also warned that such Articles will never be called into operation and that they would remain a dead letter. "I hope the President who is endowed with the power, will take proper precaution before actually suspending administration of the province."

There has been an exponential increase in the number of parties contesting elections. In the first general elections of 1952, 55 parties took part and the number jumped to 1900 in 2016, though 400 out of them have never contested any election. These dummy parties are practicing a negative brand of politics and are suspected to be conduits for turning black money into white and creating cannon fodder for political gains. Ambedkar also predicted, "In addition to our old enemies in the form of caste and creed we are going to have many political parties with divisive and opposing political creeds." Rise of multiparty coalition government further incenstivised the growth of regional parties that could wield considerable influence in the formation of government at the centre. In his farewell address to the Parliament in 2007, APJ Abdul Kalam, remarked that India has to eventually graduate to a two-party political system which he qualified as two strictly defined coalitions with pre-poll affiliations and a clear-cut development agenda.

During the national movement, Indian political leaders had a sense of service to the people. Nehru said, "They call me the Prime Minister of India, but it would be more appropriate if I were called the first servant of India." This idea was gradually lost and was replaced by a deeply feudal system. Some hold the view that *pradhan mantri, mukhya mantri* and *mantri* be renamed as *pradhan sevak, mukhya sevak* and *sevak* which embodies qualities of integrity, dedication and selfless service. Changing designation may, however, not change the basic attitude and behaviour of our politicians. What we need is *netas* who, in the words of APJ Abdul Kalam, "have courage to take difficult decisions... capable of working with integrity." He suggested that politicians should spend only 30% of their time on politics and 70% on development. Leaders today like to be on top but are reluctant to be in the front and hold the banner.

On the controversy of designations our politicians shall never converge to a point for they unanimously agree without even a minute's debate only on a topic of self-interest. Unanimity on their salary and other facilities is a significant point. During 1964-83, basic salary of an MP was rupees 500 but now they have united to push it to rupees 50,000 and are life-long pension holders. New demands have wetted their hunger and include free first-class train travel anywhere in India, not just for spouses but also for "companions". Indian MPs already rake in 68 times an average Indian's income as compared to a ratio of 35 in the US and 10 across large swathes of West Europe. Similar unity was visible when Supreme Court debarred MLAs and MPs charged in criminal cases or when an amendment to bring political parties under the ambit of RTI was tabled in Lok Sabha on August 12, 2013. The government held that bringing them under RTI Act is "flawed" on the ground that they are not constitutional bodies. They don't receive any government support and must be kept out of RTI ambit. Parties should then return land and accommodation allotted to them by the central and state governments at subsidised costs and tax concessions to political parties should also be abolished. Argument of the government is also shaky, as clubs that enjoy similar government concessions, don't have such exemptions. It is sad that democracy promises equality but its institutions continue to systematically deny it. To strengthen democracy, public pressure will be a significant factor to force political parties to be more accountable.

Apart from legislature, executive and judiciary, there are other institutions in a democracy to perform some very important functions and give a visionary direction to the democratic polity and to the working of its institutions. Most members and heads of various commissions and corporations are appointed as a consequence of their personal and unflinching political loyalty to the party in power with no evaluation of their merit or suitability. Positions are doled out to 'yes men', politicians retired from active politics or those in the sunset of their careers. Their political stripes seldom vanish as is evident from the remarks of a seasoned Congressman who after being elected as President said, "If my leader had said I should pick up a broom and be a sweeper, I would have done that. She chose me to be President." Such remarks belittle the prestige of the post and sacred principles of democracy. The Supreme Court in its judgment in 2010 observed, "Governor is the constitutional head of the state. He is not an employee or an agent of the Union government, nor a part of any political team."

Indian Constitution provides for bicameral legislature to preserve the federal structure of our country and ensure adequate representation of states in the Parliament. While Lok Sabha can be dissolved, Rajya Sabha is the permanent wing of the legislature. Its members are elected by the members of the legislative assemblies of the states and Union Territories. They have a fixed tenure of six years and one-third of its members retire after every two years. Democracies are crucially dependent on checks and balances and there are very good reasons for having a bicameral legislature, with one House representing the popular will of the day, and the other exercising restraint against a potentially hysterical mob mentality.

In theory, Rajya Sabha is supposed to represent the interests of states but in actual practice its indirect elections are akin to party nominations. Constitution framers did not visualise that Rajya Sabha will be dominated by political parties who, sacrificing the interest of the states, would hold Lok Sabha to ransom. Any political party with an absolute majority in Lok Sabha can be in an uncomfortable position in case it is in minority in Rajya Sabha. Joint session of the Parliament is then a solution. An amendment in 2003 did away with secret voting by MLAs for Rajya Sabha candidates and this has all but ensured that only party-nominated candidates win.

Some feel that the federal structure of India is sound and regional interests are adequately represented, thus rendering Rajya Sabha redundant. Political parties are simply exploiting Rajya Sabha to reward power brokers, journalists, civil servants, industrial heads, crony capitalists and losers in elections. Rajya Sabha members enjoy salaries and other benefits like Lok Sabha members and this expenditure can be gainfully deployed for other meaningful projects. Others argue that persons of lateral talent and individuals of repute inducted to bring fresh ideas and knowledge are essential. We need two significant changes to make Rajya Sabha more meaningful and constructive rather than confine it to history. Firstly, secret ballot voting for their election in states and also for their voting in Parliament with absence of issue of any whip will encourage the members to vote according to their conscience and in the interest of their state to make it truly a "state" representative body. Secondly, ministers should only be from Lok Sabha.

Indian democracy is federal in character. The word federalism is derived from the Latin word *foedus*, meaning pact or treaty. In India, its inspiration comes from the philosophy of *anekantwad*, meaning "many-sidedness". It is a philosophy that means that truth can be approached from multiple paths. It is a balance between two conflicting forces of authority and liberty. India is a vast and diverse nation where an individual state can have size and complexity of a country. This requires delegation of leadership and initiative rather than top-down command structure. A federal structure allows evolutionary dynamism and frees all constituents from unitary determinism.

Constitution framers wanted India to be a strong federal state with a tilt towards the Centre. Ambedkar said during a debate in the Constituent Assembly, "The states under the Constitution are no way dependent upon the Centre for legislation and executive authority." The framers conceived India as a federal democracy but rise of regional parties, coalition compulsions, unjustified and cynical demands, policy of obstructionism and replacing political rivalry by personal enmity have failed to provide a strong kernel and have weakened federalism. Federal structure is being damaged by creating spokes in implementing laws passed by the Centre thus putting it in grave danger and threatening its collapse. Passing of laws on a state subject marks a rupture in India's federal trajectory. A simple and politically feasible solution is decentralisation. In a law on a subject in the Concurrent List a clause may be inserted stating that the legislation shall apply to all states that do not amend it and that in the states that amend it, the amended legislation shall apply. This will unleash a spirit of competition and reform among the states and people of different cultures, ethnicity and backgrounds will be able to coexist peacefully and harmoniously. This will also encourage diversity to be a source of strength rather than weakness. Though no union is perfect, the truth is that a splintered state is not necessarily happier or more productive. With a wave of discontent in Scotland, it voted against independence and decided against breaking the 307-year-old tradition to remain a part of United Kingdom. This is a lesson for all bigger democracies especially India.

Many constitution reformers favour a change from parliamentary to presidential form of government. In the presidential form, the President is directly elected and cannot be toppled by defectors. In Presidential form there is overdependence on one man who is not a team player but an authority-figure and brooks no dissent or opposition. Political farce in US proves that presidential system can be as indecisive and corrupt as parliamentary one. There are pros and cons for both the systems. India encompasses great social, cultural, ethnic and religious diversity and with all its diversities, the collegiate prime ministerial system has largely been deemed to be more desirable and more practical. India's roots of managerial crisis lie in the mismanagement of the parliamentary system and not in any basic weakness of the system. However, a good reform of our system would be for the Parliament to elect the prime minister for a full term after every election. He can then focus on governance and resist blackmail by corrupt legislators or coalition partners. For a no-confidence motion at least 150 MPs should be required to sign instead of 50 at present. Law may be amended on the basis of 1999 Law Commission of India recommendation which has provision of a confidence motion along with a no-confidence motion so that a new government can be in place immediately in case of the incumbent losing confidence of the House as in Germany which means a government can be brought down only if there is an alternative. The solution will avoid problem of a hung parliament and horse-trading. Leader of opposition should not be leader of the largest opposition party but should be elected by all the opposition parties voting.

Indian Constitution envisaged a five-year electoral cycle and during the first four general elections simultaneous polls were held throughout the country. But this cycle was disrupted in 1969 with the premature dissolution of Lok Sabha and also due to frequent imposition of President's Rule in the states. Today throughout the year some election or the other is happening in India and the country is continuously in election mode disrupting governance. Frequent elections also cost the public exchequer more money. Elections to British Parliament, regarded as 'mother of parliaments', are held every five years on a specified date. Parliamentary Standing Committee on Personnel, Public Grievances, Law and Justice in its report in 2015 suggested a two-cycle election process. With five-year term for each, one cycle would include polls for Lok Sabha and about half the states, and the other cycle would be two-and-a-half years later for the rest of the states. Besides being less cost-effective, it would serve the fundamental democratic purpose in rendering broad public opinion to the Union government of the day and also serve the democratic principle of check and balance in the polity. If Lok Sabha or some state assemblies are dissolved in between, elections may be held only for the remaining period of the term.

Democracy, as government of the people, is supposed to ensure will of the people but Indian Parliament is not truly representative of the majority of the people. Representatives are being elected on minority votes with most candidates getting far less than 50% votes. Thus, those elected do not represent all the people and decisions by the Parliament are not will of the 'people' but only of those who voted. This defeats the very purpose of 'representative democracy'. Swiss system, where every change in law has to be approved by the people through a referendum, may be virtually impossible in India due to its vast diversities and pluralist nature. Since repeated elections will be very expensive, there can be second and third preference with system of transferable votes and the winner must get 50% votes to get elected. This will make Indian democracy more representative.

In a landmark verdict on electoral reforms to empower voters, the Supreme Court on September 27, 2013 directed the Election Commission to provide for NOTA (None of the above) option in electronic voting machines (EVMs). Though this does not affect the outcome of the contest, large disapprovals will embarrass the parties and gradually the system may change.

Dynastic feudalism, significant in Indian politics, is against the spirit of democracy. It is a political favour bestowed on the dynast and has done more harm to the growth of democracy both in the country and also in the concerned party. Having remained slaves for centuries, we are still not quite ready to wean ourselves off hero worship. We are a democracy but deep inside we prefer kings at the top. Ambedkar also said, "*Bhakti* in religion may be a road to salvation of the soul. But in politics, *bhakti* is a sure road to degradation and eventual dictatorship."

Nehru-Gandhi dynasty has ruled over Indian politics for over 60 years after independence but today the dynasty-driven Congress is confused and lacks ideas, has lost dynamism and has now completely lost direction. Some blame Nehru-Gandhi dynasty for keeping India deliberately backward in order to exploit a poor and ignorant vote-bank.

One of the reasons of the decline of Congress in Indian politics may be lack of inner-party democracy depriving more competent persons guiding its reins. Today, leadership crisis is plaguing the party and it is badly in search of some foothold. Nomination of Manmohan Singh as prime minister for two terms reveals a strong lack of desire of Congress to lead the country. Dynasty is in tatters and it is time to change the mindset, infuse internal democracy, and pass on the baton to more deserving leaders. Gandhi-*mukt* Congress may be far away but Congress-*mukt* Bharat is certainly around the corner.

Other parties in India are not free from the virus of dynastic feudalism. In these parties also, democracy is a farce and transparency a mere trifle. Of the 50 odd political parties that have some representation in Parliament or state legislatures, at least 30 are family divas. Unable to find trustworthy lieutenants, supreme leaders of such parties become acutely insecure from within and start depending upon their own progeny regardless of their inclination or ability. Dynastic politics in India is often described as a son-rise industry but in fact it may be a sun-set enterprise. It is a paradox that we demand democracy without being democrats ourselves.

There has been little objective assessment of the performance of political dynasties. Some believe that dynasts inherit administrative acumen due to their constant exposure to politics while others believe that they are helped by nepotism and by voter myopia. Research has, however, shown that MPs who belong to political dynasts with comparable MPs who do not belong to any political dynasty underperform significantly on most of the parameters. Attendance level of political dynasts in the Parliament is lower while their growth rate in crimes is higher. Afflicted with over-confidence due to their family background, they start ignoring their political duties and development suffers in their constituencies in comparison to development in non-dynast constituencies. Broadly, the results indicate that persistence of political dynasties seems to have a negative impact on economic and social performance. This is, however, not to say that all dynasts are inefficient. With all arguments in favour or against dynastic feudalism, one thing is certain that there is no dearth of talent in India and democracy is certainly a grave casualty in dynastic feudalism.

It is an irony that we are a democratic country but suffer not only from dynastic feudalism but also from inner-party democracy. Political parties have built an edifice of democracy but their foundation remains undemocratic which jeopardises their democratic credentials. Chief Ministers are appointed through a farce in the name of election after they are selected by the high command.

Besides many forces weakening the federal structure of Indian democracy, demand for more states has also been constantly affecting it. With the merger of 550 princely states after independence, reorganisation of states became imperative. In 1953, States Reorganisation Commission (SRC) recommended 16 states and 3 UTs. Language was considered to be the basis of culture and new states were created on linguistic basis. Demand for more states gained ground and Punjab, Haryana and Himachal were created in 1966, Arunachal, Meghalaya and Mizoram in 1971, and Uttarakhand (earlier called Uttaranchal) from Uttar Pradesh, Jharkhand from Bihar and Chhattisgarh from Madhya Pradesh in 2000. Telangana, the 29th baby, was born on June 2, 2014, more out of political compulsions. This has opened flood-gates for Gorkhaland in Darjeeling, Bodoland in Assam, Vidarbha from Maharashtra, and Bundelkhand out of UP and MP.

Feeling of neglect, deprivation and discrimination has led to regionalism, demand for creation of new states, and autonomy and more power to states. All these unjustified statehood demands may threaten unity and harmony of the country.

Smaller states are not ipso facto better in governance or greater in prosperity. Data and evidence show that the case for smaller or larger states, in terms of one being better than the other, is completely mixed. Performance of a state is not so much determined by its size as by the political will and orientation of its government. Smaller states certainly bring governments closer to the people and make administration easier.

Problem is not only for demand of more states but also of boundary disputes between the states. Ever since four hill states - Nagaland, Meghalaya, Arunachal Pradesh and Mizoram were carved out of Assam province, not one has come to terms with its boundaries leading to frequent clashes and encroachment claims.

Besides more states and boundary disputes, there is now demand for even caste-based crematoriums. In July 2014, Urban Improvement Trust in Jaisalmer of western Rajasthan, sanctioned and clearly marked 47 separate cremation grounds for different castes and communities. Thus, the caste tag, not dying for the living, is living for the dead also. Such increasing demands are adding to the existing diversity and threatening unity of the country.

Diversities are an integral part of India and are here to stay. Tolerance of these diversities is the strength of Indian democracy for its prosperity and its absence a grave threat to the unity of the nation and a signal for disintegration. We need strong and pragmatic leaders and a constructive opposition for far-reaching political reforms to put the already struggling democratic institutions on a smooth and solid path.

11

ROLLER COASTER RIDE

India represents a paradox. Politically it is one country but economically and socially it is a land of inequalities. Different groups anchor themselves in rigid positions and path to long-term prosperity is often in conflict with short-term goals. Political equality alone does not make a democracy strong and stable unless it is strengthened by economic and social equality.

Poverty is the greatest bane of democracy. India had made momentous progress in reducing multidimensional poverty but is still one of the poverty havens of the world. As of 2020, about 22% live below poverty line, 25.7% in rural and 13.7% in urban areas. Politicians flaunt their wealth and ironically mock at the poor by saying that rupees 32 a day is enough to see them through. A hungry person needs food and right to vote is meaningless for him. Amartya Sen, the Nobel Laureate and world-renowned economist, has rightly pointed out that hunger in India is caused by the wide prevalence of poverty. According to Global Hunger Index (GHI) data for 2017, India ranked at 100 among 119 countries on the basis of undernourishment and child mortality. It is optimistically believed that extreme poverty in India could be eliminated altogether by 2030. This will need high GDP growth rate and sharp increase in wages.

While economic growth has been there in India, disparity is increasing. Inequality in distribution of economic resources is extremely glaring. In terms of wealth, India has seen a whopping 211% increase in its wealth over the last 15 years. India is now the tenth richest country in the world, ranked according to total private wealth held by all individuals. Wealth is, however, getting skewed towards the richest. Income of the richest 10% increased by 15% while that of the poorest 10% decreased by over 15%. India's richest hold 58% of the country's total wealth and just 57 billionaires have the same wealth as the bottom 70% population. Lack of basic social needs like nutrition, health care and education have further widened the disparity between the rich and the poor.

Regarding assets, average assets of the richest 10% in urban population are rupees 14.6 crore while for poorest 10% they are rupees 291. Similarly, for richest 10% in rural population they are rupees 5.7 crore and for poorest 10% are rupees 2,507. Increase in slum population, from 1.3 crore in 2011 to 10.4 crore in 2017, coupled with increase in crimes and social tensions, has further added to socio-economic inequality.

Journey of economic development in India during the last seven decades has been a roller coaster ride.

Industrial policy was announced in April 1948 which was far from being radical. Industries like atomic energy, armaments and railways were state-owned and were called "public" sector and expansion of steel, coal, mines, shipyard, and post and telegraph were to be handled by the state. Remaining industries were placed under "private" sector with highly centralised rules and procedures. Economic development suffered heavily for the next four decades due to absence of liberal expansion of industry. Socialist and mixed economy prevailed from 1950 to 1979 and Nehru-Indira socialist model placed India in economic decline. Investment was concentrated on infrastructure and heavy industry which had to rely heavily on foreign aid and import of foreign machinery. Compulsive need of India to arm against the growing menace of China created hurdles and development soon went off the rails. Industrial growth declined and foreign exchange was virtually down to nil. Living standard of the people was pathetic and income per head per day was meager 72 paise. Life expectancy was only 27 years and literacy rate 17%, with over two million unemployed and about 15 million underemployed. Scarcity of food was a grave problem and only one out of hundred villages had electric power. Agriculture was stagnant, production fell and India had to import food grain. Population was growing at the rate of 2.5% per year and with barely 2.4% of the world's land surface, India had to support over 14% of world population. No efforts were made to check population explosion as population control was not a vote catcher. This lapse has negated all the meagre social and economic developments during the last seven decades. Nehru remarked in 1948, "The question of limiting the family is not the primary question. We have to make economic progress much more rapidly…" It is unfortunate that neither economic growth could take place nor population could be controlled. Nehru is often blamed for initiating wrong economic policies and not considering economic liberalisation as an option. Later global developments are ample testimony to his failure as an economist. Other countries changed course with the passage of time whereas he and his successors failed to do so. The blame lies more squarely on the short-sightedness of his successors.

Shastri inherited grave economic crisis from Nehru but as a far-sighted man of iron will and full of common sense he handled all problems with great maturity. He contemplated liberalisation and deregulated industrial economy as he realised that controls were a waste. The sensational and bold "Green Revolution" policy initiated by him ushered in an era of agricultural expansion and transformed India from a food deficient country to a food surplus one. India was in such a strong position in 1980 that it could donate food to Ethiopia and give wheat loan to Vietnam. His mysterious end cut short the growing prospects of India's economic development.

Indira Gandhi who succeeded Shastri was by nature more bureaucratic, authoritarian and stubborn. Not pragmatic in economic reforms, she buried all initiatives of liberalisation, discouraged foreign investment and placed more hurdles on domestic enterprise. No export-oriented policies were introduced and no liberal economic models were adopted. She favoured licencing and excessive regulation. Productivity declined due to poor investment in infrastructure. *'Garibi hatao'* remained only a hollow slogan and a vote-catching device.

Indira Gandhi brought legislative changes to protect organised labour by forbidding lay-off of workers in firms with 100 or more workers. Tough and restrictive labour laws protected the workers but created obstacles in the expansion of industries. Trade unions became more powerful and politicians were unwilling to control them for the fear of displeasing their large and powerful vote-bank. Work ethics declined and productivity tumbled.

Social protection of workers is a desirable outcome of democracy but it was pushed too far at the cost of cheap popularity. Workers may be protected but employers must be allowed to 'hire and fire' them. John P Lewis, an American economist wrote in his book 'Quiet Crisis in India' that social protection of workers is good from humanitarian point of view but India's capacity to export at competitive prices may be gravely undermined as a result of spiraling wages unaccompanied by equivalent productivity increases. In the interest of workers and welfare of the nation, solution lies in junking labour norms that discourage enterprise from expanding and in investing in workers' training.

In pursuance of her socialist policies, Indira Gandhi imposed a ceiling of thirty acres on holding of land. Possibility of economic reforms was further crippled by the nationalisation of banks that were regarded as 'monopoly capitalists' controlled by a handful of big houses that ran their business only for the welfare of their families. Monopolies and Restrictive Trade Practices (MRTP) Act was enacted in 1969 by which any group with combined assets of above rupees 20 crores or a single company with assets more than one crore was declared a "monopoly" and effectively debarred from expanding its business. The policy termed as "one of the most damaging in modern Indian history" strangulated business initiative and economic growth further declined. Finally, in September 1991, the Narasimha Rao government scrapped this ridiculous law.

Like Nehru, Indira Gandhi was also a socialist at heart and her distaste for capitalism throttled economic enterprise. She did not favour market-based models being followed in other parts of the world and doors to foreign investors were completely shut due to her political activism. Even local enterprise was chocked due to extreme protectionism. Heavy handed controls consumed more foreign exchange and for 29 years out of 35 from 1956, India faced acute problem of balance-of-payment.

An array of permits and licences stifled business initiative and created mistrust for future business. On account of stringent and anti-development economic policies, many industrialists turned towards other countries and established their factories there due to economic liberalisation in those countries. Shrewd businessmen, like Dhirubhai Ambani, managed contacts with people close to Indira Gandhi and made a complete mockery of the corrupt regime. Eminent economists also preferred to leave rather than bang their heads against the wall of intellectual bankruptcy. Persons like Manmohan Singh continued to serve the limping system due to their lack of courage to oppose the government policies. Economic loss due to extreme protectionist policies cannot be quantified.

No attention was paid to the development of infrastructure. Roads, ports and bridges were over-crowded and harbours were unable to cope with even the meagre volume of imports and exports. Irrigation and power were totally neglected and "load-shedding" was a regular feature in all cities. There was also derailment in the eradication of poverty, universalisation of education and other democratic ideals for social development. This period is characterised as 'Quota- Permit-Licence (QPL) Raj'. In 1977, Janta government under Morarji Desai appointed a "committee on controls and subsidies" to analyse QPL. The government fell and recommendations of the committee could not be implemented.

Indira Gandhi returned as PM for a second tenure in 1980 and initiated a clear reversal of her own failed policies of socialist era. She handled recession, drought and famine problems rather effectively. Still, no liberal economic reforms were initiated. Industrial growth plunged from 7.7% between 1951 and 1965 to 4% between 1966 and 1980. India was worst performer among developing countries and the period of three decades is termed as "dark period of Indian economy". It was with gradual abandonment of Nehruvian socialism that Indian growth accelerated and welfare gap between India and rest of the world started closing.

Nehru-Gandhi dynasty that ruled India for 37 of its first 42 years after independence presided over one of Asia's greatest economic flops. When Rajiv Gandhi took over as prime minister, the whole economy was mired in mess. Business enterprises that contribute over 50% to GDP, a term now used as a more effective summary measure of welfare, were forced to hide their earnings and avoid payment of taxes, duties and levies due to outdated laws. To enhance revenues and to minimise temptation for black money, tax rates have to be moderate and laws simple to mitigate the temptation to evade. Rajiv Gandhi was sincerely keen to solve the perennial problems of Indian economy and tried to bring in an era of radical economic reforms by deviating from five-year plans and 'permit *raj*'. He introduced 'New Economic Policy' in 1985. Some taxes were cut, quotas freed and licencing requirements reduced or simplified. Economic growth broke the barrier of 3-3.5 and rose to 5.5. He favoured liberalisation and encouraged private investment from both India and abroad. He adopted modern technology, spearheaded

India's computerisation programme and took dramatic measures to take the nation to the twenty-first century. Unable to make any deep dent in the economic development he expressed his helplessness when he said that for every one rupee sent to the common man, only 17 paise reached him. Old guards tried to tie his hands by arguing that liberalisation would lead to inequitable reforms and create an imbalance in the society. Economic liberalisation was stifled and timid Rajiv failed to implement modern liberal economic policies.

With the vast majority in the Parliament on his side Rajiv Gandhi could have revolutionalised the fate of the nation but he wasted the opportunity. Bofors guns turned out to be the biggest crisis ever faced by any government in the past and Rajiv Gandhi soon got mired in political and scam mess. Destiny cut short his life in the prime of his political career.

With the death of Rajiv Gandhi era of economic reforms was born. Narasimha Rao took the path of liberalisation in 1991 out of compulsion and not conviction. Ideas and radical approach came from Manmohan Singh, his finance minister, but it was Rao who made it politically feasible in spite of severe resistance from within the Congress party. Red-tapism, long delays, hassles and corruption that had seeped into the business systems were consumed to dustbin. Licence *raj* was done away with and everything was open except a small negative list relating to security and environment.

Revolutionary reforms of Rao brought the fiscal deficit down from 8.4% of GDP in 1990-91 to 5.7% in 1992-93. Foreign exchange reserves shot up to $20 billion from $1 billion in July 1991 and inflation came down to 6% from 13% in mid-1993. The New Industrial Policy of July 24, 1991 which opened door to direct foreign investment was his brain-child. Procedures for FDI approvals were considerably simplified and foreign companies that had left, started returning. Foreign investment in India increased from $132 million in 1991-92 to $5.3 billion by 1995-96. Industrial licencing was decreased with only 18 industries subject to it. Custom duty was reduced from a peak of 200% in 1991 to 40% by mid-nineties and excise duty was also reduced. Tax rates were reduced from 56% in 1991 to 40% by 1993 and to 30% in 1997. Lowering taxes did not reduce the government revenues and in fact increased it due to the broadening of the base. Indian companies were now allowed to borrow from abroad through global depository receipts. Large industrial houses were free from the much despised MRTP Act and markets grew due to increase in demand. Electric power, airlines, banking, petroleum and cellular phones were freed from public sector monopoly and came within the folds of private sector. Easing of government control in service sector like communication and insurance, and entry of private enterprise in infrastructure, aviation and telecom led to rapid growth in output. Condition of telephone sector was woeful with a paltry 2.8 million telephones and millions in an eight-year waiting list. As a result of liberalisation, 20 million telephone connections were provided with no waiting list.

Besides economic development Narasimha Rao government actively pursued agenda for elimination of poverty and promotion of education. Some of the laudable schemes were, opening ration shops in drought-prone areas, deserts, hills and tribal areas, and national old-age pension scheme, national family benefit scheme to help BPL families in case of death of bread-earner, national maternity benefit scheme for BPL families, mid-day meal programme to improve malnutrition and increase school attendance, employment assurance scheme to provide guaranteed employment in the poorest districts of the country, and *Rashtriya Mahila Kosh* to provide financial support to working women. All this turn-around in economic and social development is one of the fastest recoveries in recent times and consumed to dust the socialism of Nehru, Indira, and Rajiv.

After years of political turmoil, Atal Bihari Vajpayee was sworn in as the head of a coalition government, called National Democratic Alliance (NDA). He was the second great reformist prime minister of India after Narasimha Rao and carried forward the reforms initiated by him. Both were not economists but provided the politically desired leadership. Growth during NDA government is more impressive and deserves much applause. Vajpayee government tried to free the dwindling economy from a corrupt and bloated public sector and initiated liberalisation of most state corporations, including

Videsh Sanchar Nigam Limited. Special export processing zones, Information Technology, and Industrial Parks were established across the country to bolster industrial production. His telecom policy replaced fixed licences with revenue sharing that led to India's mobile phone revolution. He launched the National Highway Development Project and *Pradhan Mantri Gram Sadak Yojna.* In his tenure were developed half the roads developed in the earlier 32 years. Banking, insurance, public sector enterprise, foreign trade and investment, direct and indirect taxes, agricultural produce marketing, small-scale industries, ports, electricity, petroleum prices, and interest rates were areas of far-reaching reforms during his tenure. His civil aviation policy boosted competition and improved travel experience for millions of passengers. These reforms improved the economic health of the country and promoted productivity and growth. India's import rose from 8.3% of GDP in 1990 to 19.3% in 2004. Growth shifted to above 8.5% in the last fiscal year of his tenure and remained there for almost a decade. *Shiksha Abhiyan* was another flagship programme for universalisation of primary education "in a time bound manner". *Antodaya Anna Yojna,* was launched in December 2000 to provide highly subsidised food to millions of poorest families. Revolutionary economic reforms during the last decade of the century created record wealth, and also reduced poverty by a record 138 million people thereby making a concerted effort to smoothen to some extent the pits created in the path of democracy during the earlier four decades.

Ironically, two non-economist prime ministers revolutionised economic reforms while Manmohan Sing, one of the ablest economist prime minister, who succeeded Atal Bihari Vajpayee and who had brought about great economic reforms as finance minister under Narasimha Rao, wavered and failed in further strengthening Indian economy. By the time UPA limped out of office – battered by corruption, scandals and lackluster growth – India had come to be seen as one of the world's "fragile five" economies.

During UPA regime, spate of corruption scandals resulted in diversion from economic reforms. Just as diabetes affects every part of human body, lack of constructive governance lead to decline in every aspect of social, economic and political system. Growth nosedived from over 8.5% to 5.5%, industrial output slowed to a twenty-year low of 1% and the fiscal deficit increased from 3.97% to 8.10% of GDP. Subsidies were more than 2.5% of GDP and a third of the budget was spent on welfare schemes that were mostly pilfered. Out of every hundred rupees that made up the Centre's income, 37% were spent on debt and 33% on subsidies and pension. Government turned a deaf ear to slash subsidies, hasten disinvestment, streamline social programmes and show political commitment to implement long-overdue reforms. The incompetent UPA-2 did nothing apart from making a few pious statements. People were frustrated due to economic decline, inflation, unchecked and rampant corruption, and silent complacency of the government. A government that reduces food on the plate of the poor is irresponsible.

Controversial tax laws and policy paralysis after a series of scandals scared the foreign investors. India's ranking among nations by inflation rate plunged to 142 out of 153 emerging markets. Business confidence faltered due to stubborn prices, high interest rates, slackening in exports and decline in private investment. GDP and industrial growth rate slumped lowest in a decade. World GDP also declined steadily from 5.3% in 2010 to 2.9% in the next three years but India had gone downhill much faster than other developing countries due to economic mismanagement. No sustained efforts were made to lift the economic growth rate and Indian economy could never come out of the woods.

The record of UPA from 2004 to 2014 is not very progressive and the high growth during this period was the accumulation of reforms undertaken by India's two great prime ministers, PV Narasimha Rao and Atal Bihari Vajpayee. Decision-making paralysis under UPA-2 significantly contributed to slowdown from 2009 to 2014. Inequality, lack of infrastructure and education-deficiencies continued to be key weaknesses. It failed in the task of building highways and rural roads, reforming electricity sector, labour and land markets, and higher education. Social programmes that empower people, particularly women, were ignored. Lapses of UPA may be difficult to be remedied.

Manmohan Singh's period of premiership is essentially a story of economic mismanagement, joblessness and inability to tame rampant inflation. The buoyant prime minister promised the nation from the ramparts of Red Fort in 2005 that poverty and ignorance would end in 10 years. Nine years later, on the same day from the same place he admitted that there was a long way to go.

UPA government focused more on "inclusive growth" which is growth in labour-intensive manufacturing and not on "inclusive spending" which is judicious use of ever-rising revenues. Poverty, ill health and illiteracy can be eradicated only when both processes work hand-in-hand. India also failed to do any nuclear business with other nations due to tough nuclear liability laws. Top industrialists invested only in highly capital-intensive sectors such as automobiles, engineering goods and chemicals or in skilled-labour-intensive goods like software, telecommunications, finance and pharmaceuticals. The government did not create conditions for setting up large-scale industries in labour-intensive products.

Nationalisation of companies resulted in huge national loss. Hindustan Fertilizer at Haldia (West Bengal) was set up in 1986 at the cost of $1.2 billion and had 1500 employees. After seven years it did not produce even a single kilo of fertilizer. Similarly, Scooter India

Limited at Lucknow had not built even a single scooter for 10 years paying wages to over 3000 workers. Steel Authority of India paid wages to 247,000 workers to produce 6 million tons whereas Pohan Steel Company in South Korea produced 14 million tons in the same year with only 10,000 employees. Some PSUs like ONGC and SAIL are examples of success but most are bleeding cash for decades. Air India is suffering loss every year and has a debt of around rupees 60,000 crore. Subsequently, NITI Aayog recommended its closure or sell-off besides 74 other loss-making PSUs. It is estimated that in "organised sector" over 70% of the employees alone received their pay-cheques without contributing anything. The government decided to shut down 15 loss-making public sector units but their fate has remained uncertain amid hectic lobbying by ministries and bureaucracy with government's "hands tied behind its back".

For equitable distribution of opportunities society has to provide reasonable economic assistance to the poor and socially deprived to bring them as close to the top as possible. Due to vote-bank politics Congress resorted to populist giveaways, and expensive and leaky social welfare programmes like loan waivers, subsidies and freebees. They are laudable social schemes for the poor but in the long run deleterious to social, economic and democratic health of the nation. Loan waivers unfairly benefit those with best access to banking system. The poor and low caste peasants are forced to take shelter with loans from private money lenders at high rates of interest. Loan waivers further widen fiscal deficit and in 2008 alone it was rupees 60,000 crore. Unless controlled, this could spin into complete doom.

Like loan waivers, subsidies also benefit upper class. It is estimated that top 20% of households capture six times more in benefits from fuel subsidies than the poorest 20%. In 2012-13, the government collected rupees 98,603 crore as taxes from petroleum products while simultaneously handed out a little over rupees one trillion as subsidies to the petroleum sector. It is better to reduce taxes on petrol and diesel by phasing out diesel subsidies. Same is the case of rich farmers who draw more benefit on fertilizers than the poor. Besides these, subsidies on free electricity to all farmers, subsidised food in Parliament canteens, airport privileges and widespread tax breaks to parliamentarians, are all unwarranted. Amount spent on subsidies could be invested in factories, roads, schools, hospitals, irrigation and power projects to create more jobs. For equitable social justice subsidies to BPL families may be through cash transfers into the bank account of the female head of the household via mobile banking. The road to equitable prosperity, however, lies through jobs and not giveaways. There is a saying that if you give a fish to a man one day, he will come next day for more; if you teach him to fish he will be independent. We must resist the temptation to turn populist and think whether we want long-term prosperity or the path of short-term populist giveaways.

Freebees that have exponentially increased during the last few decades are another significant vote catching device. Ahead of polls, political parties weave big dreams and lure poor, ignorant and grieving masses with freebees like booze, power, TV sets, computers, mixers, grinders, fans, gold, *mangalsutras, sarees* and a host of other things along with subsidised food, loan waivers, NREGA jobs, cash transfers and caste reservations. All these false promises are back-rolled after coming to power. Culture of freebees starves economic growth, creates laziness among the youth that kills their work-culture, and reduces industrial production. It is like distribution of free sweets that is initially attractive but finally destroys the health of the individual.

In 2013 SC directed the Election Commission to consult political parties to frame model code of conduct so that they do not announce freebees in their manifesto to lure voters. Political parties argue that poll promises or "freebees" are related to Directive Principles of State Policy. Election Commission must come out with a pragmatic set of guidelines that would allow freebees as long as they are targeted at the economically and socially weaker sections, women, and population living in border or insurgency/disaster hit areas. Political parties should also be held accountable for non-fulfillment of their hollow poll-promises.

By these senseless policies those at the bottom of the social heap suffered due to poor implementation and the middle class was also alienated from Congress. Another glaring example of turning populist, based on the futile notion that two or more wrongs always make a right, is legalisation of illegal colonies that have mushroomed on government land in every corner of the country. All political parties are in a scramble to regularise these irregular colonies. Their demolition becomes a political issue and courts also generally stay such demolitions due to social compulsions. Encroachment on government land is not only by public but also by political parties for their offices and residences. All these undemocratic policies weaken the edifice of Indian democracy and do not usher in prosperity. Pranab Mukherjee said in his Republic Day-eve speech in January 2014, "Government is not a charity shop. Populist anarchy cannot be a substitute for governance."

With dismal record in implementing reforms, some steps were taken by UPA to rebuild confidence in economy. Conducive tax environment was created to attract FDI. In July 2013 doors were opened to greater foreign investment in about a dozen sectors. FDI limit was hiked from 74% to 100% in telecom, 26% to 49% in insurance, 49% in petroleum and natural gas refining, and 49% in single brand retail in defence production. This helped contain deficit that had gone up to 4.8% of GDP. FDI inflow soon slowdown due to amendments in policies and tax structures, some of them retrospectively, that shattered investor confidence. India's FDI stock as a percentage of GDP was at 12.2% in contrast to 30.4% for developing economies.

Opposition's negative attitude that FDI in multi-brand retail will lead to closure of small shops has no rationale. Closure of some shops is compensated by creation of alternative jobs, reduction in price by foreign-owned chains and raise in living standard of people. Some obstructionists argue that technology will create huge job loss. It may create some job loss but it increases productivity and creates jobs elsewhere. Computers have displaced millions of clerical jobs and cell phones have killed the camera industry but have created jobs in other technical sectors. Besides, foreign companies contribute to tax revenues, and bring in technology and best management practices. Constant uprooting of existing forms of work, occupations, and social and industrial organisations are the 'creative destructions' which are constantly smashing the existing systems to create new and better ones. Only an industrial revolution can bring an economic revolution and make India prosperous.

As a poll gimmick, UPA government introduced NREGA in 2005. The scheme guaranteed 100 days of wage-employment in a financial year on a pre-specified minimum wage to one adult per rural household to do unskilled manual work. This pro-poor scheme had laudable social objective but badly devised and poorly implemented. The manual work given is simply to dig new watering sets every time one is cleaned away in monsoon. The notoriously ill-conceived scheme with multi-crore fraud is devoid of any skill learning or job creation. It is dubbed by economists as world's most corrupt institution.

Food Security Bill promised freedom from hunger and chronic malnutrition by supplying 5 kg of cereal per person per month while the average consumption of cereal in the country is 10.7 kg/pppm. Law is enacted on the ridiculous assumption that 66% of Indians go hungry to bed when less than 2% claim to be hungry according to official surveys. Full year cost of this bill, including storage and transportation, was not below rupees 2 lakh crore a year, up from current food subsidy of rupees 75,000 crore in 2012-13. Political parties supported it without any discussion for vote-bank politics.

Public Distribution System (PDS) of the subsidised food was plagued by high leakage, operating cost and corruption. It cost rupees 3.65 to deliver food worth rupee one and 57% of the subsidised grains did not reach target groups. Farmers sold their produce to the government, say wheat at Rs. 14/kg and then asked the government to give them back the same at rupees 2/kg. It was absurd. It would have been better to give them cash support instead. There are 147 centrally sponsored social schemes that have not achieved desired outcomes over the years. All such leaky schemes must be scrapped and phased out. The agenda is big but all long-term problems can be addressed by pragmatic short-term steps by an optimist, strong and determined leadership to achieve their potential.

Instead of leaky and cheap vote catching schemes, India needs urgent agriculture reforms. Unseasonal rains and hailstorms damage standing crops and farmers commit suicide mainly due to bankruptcy and non-payment of loans. Agricultural Produce Marketing Committees (APMC), which function as wholesale carters in *mandis* need to be scrapped. This will bring competition as traders and farmers will be able to buy and sell freely and international traders will be able to buy directly from farmers. This will result in higher return to farmers and also lower prices for consumers. Crop insurance, better irrigation schemes, 61.3 million tons of cold storage against present 29 million tones and new technology are urgently needed. The minimum support price system needs to be rationalised. Progressive farm laws had to be repealed due to obstructionist tendency of the opposition and lobbying of a section of farmers from a small part of the country. Serious effort of social reforms becomes a casualty due to such undemocratic approach of an obstructionist minority.

Employment and job creation have been the greatest banes of our economic policies. According to Economic Survey findings, total employment in the country grew by just 1.6% per year from 1999 to 2009 and UPA created only an abysmal 2.7 million jobs as against 60.7 million created under NDA. UPA also failed to come to grips with creeping inflation and stubborn levels of inequality. In 2017 India ranked 132 out of 152 countries on their commitment on reducing inequality. Income inequality doubled during UPA regime particularly after 2013, thus weakening one of the strongest pillars of democracy.

With its dismal record in economic and social developments, UPA introduced some valuable reforms to eliminate leakages and usher in transparency. Direct Cash Transfer (DCT) scheme and *'Aapka paisa, aapke haath'* that transferred to bank account of the beneficiary in lieu of subsidy, scholarships, pensions and MNREGA was an innovative idea. Scheme of the government to allocate rupees 5 crore every year to each MP for infrastructure projects in their constituency under the 'MP Local Area Development Scheme', (MPLADS) is laudable.

Enactment of Right to Information Act, 2005 was a significant contribution towards promoting greater accountability. It is a game changer and is India's sunshine law that provides access to information and opportunities. Information is power and RTI is a veritable *'Brahmastra'* in the hands of Indian public.

Modi made economy and development primary election issues and pronounced 'minimum government, maximum governance' as his slogan. He is a visionary and wants to make "development" a *'jan andolan'*, a mass movement. His most cherished aim is to create an environment for economic growth and job opportunities. His new financial inclusion push, named *Pradhan Mantri Jan Dhan Yojna*, aims at direct cash transfer in bank of the beneficiary and is a more efficient, less corrupt way to deliver welfare and slash leakages.

Schemes like *'Swachh Bharat'* and construction of toilets in villages will go a long way in strengthening our social systems. In growth and development, small steps lead to big leaps. Digitisation and submission of information online are imperative tools for administrative transparency and efficiency. E-governance ensures efficient storage and retrieval of data, enhanced access to government agencies and efficient service delivery. To modernise our system it is essential to get rid of the cumbersome processes that are an impediment to decision-making and are not a support. Serious endeavour is essential to reduce delays in actions that cause delay in decisions. Reduction in paper work has been implemented to a very large extent and is continuing at a very fast pace. Similarly, it is feasible and desirable to build an online index that may track daily life problems like status of passport, driving licence, power connection, admissions in schools and colleges, water and power supply, FIRs and feedback on complaints. Access to public and bureaucratic action and records has been safeguarded to a great extent by the Right to Information Act. There is no dearth of things the state can do to ease daily life in governance-parched India. Small smooth footpaths will level the path of democracy leading to greater prosperity. Pace of change is always slow but must be steady. Change is a clear writing on the wall and India now no longer lives in information blackout.

When Narendra Modi became Prime Minister, his first remarks to Parliament were that the era of poverty alleviation was over and that age of poverty elimination had begun. Planning Commission, set up in 1950 was a relic of the socialist era. Rajiv Gandhi dismissed the body of Planning Commission as a "bunch of jokers". It was only in his last year as Prime Minister that Manmohan Singh asked the Planning Commission to introspect. It has now been replaced by NITI Aayog or National Institution for Transforming India. Headed by the Prime Minister, it has a governing council comprising CMs of all states, Lt. Governors of Union Territories, 7-8 full time members, four Union ministers as ex-officio members and two part-time members from leading universities and research organisations. It has a vice-chairman and CEO to be appointed by the PM.

The key objective of NITI Aayog is to "foster cooperative federalism" for providing a "national agenda" to the Centre and the states where reforms take root and results show. Earlier Centre was often seen as "giver" and states as "recipients". NITI Aayog has changed that equation and forged an equal relationship between the centre and the states.

Goods and Services Tax (GST), introduced in India from July, 2017, is a 'game changer' towards economic reform. Taxation system in India consists of direct and indirect taxes. Income tax paid by an individual is a direct tax. Sale tax, services tax and central excise tax are examples of indirect taxes paid at every stage from the time of production. This leads to paying tax over tax and hence makes the cost of production very high. GST was conceived to unify the entire country into one single market with a destination-based taxation to eliminate many indirect taxes and to introduce a single goods and services tax in the country.

In the world of economics where controlled experiments are not possible, the only guide to the success of new policies is international precedent. France was the first country to implement GST. Today more than 165 countries have already implemented it. In India it was initially considered almost 30 years back and Congress government first proposed its introduction in April 2010 but BJP opposed it only due to political obstructionism. When BJP came to power in 2014, it introduced and passed it in Lok Sabha but now Congress stalled its passage in Rajya Sabha. After lot of see-saw battle and constitutional formalities, the four GST legislations were finally approved on 29th March, 2017. It has put Indian economy on high-growth trajectory and ushered in transparency, efficiency, competency in business environment, and facilitated doing business.

Green revolution in 1960s and revolution in information technology and telecom sectors at the end of last century were significant mile-stones in the socio-economic progress of India. Now there is desperate need to unleash manufacturing revolution to find meaningful employment for the young population. Making land easily available, junking restrictive labour laws and creating a small business innovation fund are necessary conditions for labour-intensive manufacturing to take off in India. Launch of the ambitious 'Make in India' and '*Local ko vocal*' campaigns of BJP government to ease business and promote manufacturing will yield laudable results if implemented vigorously. China's rising wages can provide India with a special window of opportunity to commence a manufacturing revolution. The next 20 years are India's opportunity to create more jobs and skill the people in manufacturing sector.

Inequality continues to be a persistent issue in our larger socio-economic landscape. Our shaky economy needs to improve governance, introduce a medium to long-term fiscal policy framework, increase trade with neighbours, liberalise financial markets, innovate in farming and energy, streamline interest rates, build more infrastructure and protect the environment. Slogans will not deliver, we have to walk the talk.

Environment for doing business in India is challenging for overseas companies, given multiplicity of approvals and unpredictable policy regime. Other competitive countries have a 'single window clearance' for starting a business while our red tape creates all sorts of hindrances. Raghuram Rajan, former Governor of Reserve Bank also says that the solution is to boost investment, create a transparent and honest system of clearance, and slash the jungle of controls designed to the holy name of socialism, tribal welfare, environmental welfare and other sacred cows that hamper business. To shore up shaky investor confidence, it is vital that laws be changed prospectively and not retrospectively. According to International Finance Corporation's (IFC), India ranked 130 out of 190 countries in 2017 in the ease of doing business. It is paradoxical that an authoritarian country, like China, is friendlier to business than a democracy.

A progressive human society has to meet the basic needs of its citizens to evolve and sustain their quality of life and create conditions for all individuals to reach their full potential. Besides economic reforms, social reforms have also been gravely neglected by the custodians of our democracy. Right to life provided in our Constitution is undoubtedly the most fundamental of all rights as all other rights will have no value if there is no life. Sadly, healthcare in India is a story of insufficient resources and poor outcomes. India is short of 3 million doctors and 6 million nurses. In rural India around 30% of rural population has to travel over 30 km for treatment and women deliver babies on the road due to lack of transport facilities. Average life expectancy in India has, however, jumped up to 66.1 years but mortality rate is 42 per 1,000 live births. Insurance coverage is also abysmal with just around 25% of the population covered.

India currently spends a little over 1% of GDP on health which is among the lowest in the world. Its per capita public expenditure on health increased from rupees 621 in 2009 to rupees 1,112 ($ 16.8) in 2015-16 while Switzerland spends $ 6944 and US $4802. India plans to launch its ambitious National Health Protection Scheme (NHPS), *Ayushman Bharat Yojna*, popularly known as Modicare, to cover over 10 crore poor families with an annual health cover of rupees 5 lakh per family.

Housing and environmental conditions continue to be equally pathetic. Majority of people, both rural and urban, live in homes with space smaller than the minimum floor area of 96 sq. ft. recommended for prison cells. Air pollution is a significant cause of health damage. In 2014, India was ranked 174 among 178 in air pollution study. Delhi, the second most populated city in the world, has been ranked as the most polluted city. Out of 20 most polluted cities in the world 13 are in India. It is unfortunate that serious and life-threatening concerns like pollution and environment do not attract the attention of our political leaders as they are not their vote banks.

Education, one of the strongest pillars of a developing democracy, is another neglected area. A shocking reality is that over 8.4 crore children are out of school, 78 lakh are forced to earn a livelihood even before they attend school and 82.2 lakh work as child labourers.

In literacy, India lags behind most of the world though male literacy rate is said to be 82% and female 65%. According to Census 2011 data, 20% of the age group covered under the RTE Act does not go to school. According to a UNESCO report of 2016, India will achieve universal primary education by 2050, universal lower secondary education in 2060 and universal upper secondary education in 2085. Education remains one of the most significant causes of a weak democracy and corrupt political institutions that have eroded democracy.

India's problem is not just illiteracy and disastrous school education but also an abysmal university system. While the world has moved to greater autonomy and institutional freedom in education, Indian universities remain hostage to political and bureaucratic whims and the government's micro-managing education still fits the pattern of socialist-era.

With the proliferation of quota system for admission, the overall quality of future IIT graduates is bound to decline. Even IIT Delhi, one of the most prestigious institutions of India, was ranked as low as 172 in World University Ranking in 2018. As we tried to reach education to the lowest common denominator, we constantly lowered standards so that the weakest could catch up. Average intellectual capacity of our nation today is determined not by our brightest but by our dumbest. It is time to liberalise higher education and encourage institutional autonomy and creativity to keep pace with a rapidly changing world. Those who cannot compete for higher education and fall off the education pyramid must be accommodated in the job market. In India only 3.5% of the workforce is skilled compared to 46% in China, 74% in Germany and 96% in Korea.

Road of Indian democracy had pitfalls, bumps, speed-breakers and wide ditches right from the very beginning. Other democracies have faced similar problems but have reformed their institutions. Conventional wisdom goes that all economic and social reforms need to be introduced in India by stealth in small incremental changes that are less painful and better shock-absorbers. India can be a global power but there is no consensus among political parties on social and economic reforms. This has given our democracy a grave setback in its development. Indian democracy must move on a path of sustainable development, harmonious and directed towards improvement of life. Focus should be on removal of poverty, ignorance, discrimination and unemployment. In India the lamp of democracy has never shown with any great conviction. Our politicians, generation after generation, have paid no heed to the glaring problem of economic and social inequality. India needs to strengthen its democratic institutions else we fall by the wayside. The window of opportunity is narrow but what's visible through it is an expansive horizon.

12

PEBBLES AND BOULDERS

Historically women have generally been discriminated against in all countries and in all ages. Social status has considerably improved with time but in some societies and cultures it continues to be deplorable. Gender equality is one of the basic principles of democracy. Article 15(1) of the Indian Constitution that deals with fundamental right to non-discrimination says, "The State shall not discriminate against any citizen on grounds only of religion, race, caste, sex, place of birth or any of them." Unfortunately, some part of this promise is yet to be redeemed and women empowerment still remains an unfulfilled dream. Increasing violence against women and children is also on the rise in India. Seventy years of freedom has seen abduction of women increase by 380%, kidnapping by 750%, and rape by a whopping 870%. There is exponential rise of child rape cases by 336% and rape by juveniles by 143% from 2004 to 2013. India is dubbed as the world's most unsafe countries for women and a woman is raped somewhere in India every 20 minutes. The data also records an increase of total cognisable crimes from 18.3 per one lakh population in 2004 to 26.5 per one lakh population in 2013.

In India, crimes against women have risen noticeably but rape is still the most under-reported crime. Sadly, false rape cases, particularly by greedy middle-class women for extortion of money, greed for property, defaming the victim, and other similar reasons, are also on the rise. Conviction rate for rape is 26% and is abysmally low. Acid attacks are other vicious, potentially life-threatening crimes. For the healthy growth of democracy, it is essential to treat the safety of women on top priority.

In India, we worship Durga, Kali, Lakshmi and Saraswati, all female forms of divinity. Our ancient philosophy also believes *Yatra naryasya poojjyante, ramante tatra devta* - gods reside where women are worshipped. Woman was always held in high esteem but molestation, rape and gang-rape tarnished her image in course of time and today there is none to listen to her woes, leave aside protecting her.

On the night of December 16, 2012, Jyoti Sing, a 23-year-old paramedic student, given a symbolic name 'Nirbhaya', was brutally assaulted and gang-raped in a bus by a gang of five men and a 17-year old. Admitted to a Delhi hospital and then taken to Singapore, she died there 13 days after her rape.

'Nirbhaya' died but her death sparked unprecedented deep agony among the people and drove an anguished citizenry onto the streets against this dastardly and horrific crime. Protests continuously gained strength and vehemently conveyed a loud "enough is enough" message. Due to pressure of public, a fast-track court awarded death sentence to four accused, one committed suicide inside the jail and the juvenile was sentenced to a maximum of three years in a reformation home by the Juvenile Justice Board. Peoples' movement engendered by this tragedy persuaded Parliament to amend existing laws against sexual violence and juveniles involved in heinous crimes to make them more stringent. Lok Sabha passed a bill to amend the Juvenile Justice Board Act to try juveniles aged 16-18 years who commit heinous crimes like rape or murder as adults. Public pressure is a testimony to the fact that people, if united, can awaken the government from deep slumber and strengthen democracy. In India democracy is safe in the hands of a united and vigilant citizenry.

Rash, undignified, vulgar and puerile statements on rape from politicians have been shocking. During the parliamentary debate on rape laws, president of a political party loudly asserted that there is no man who has not pursued a woman. President of another political party publicly declared that "boys will be boys". His remark that rape by four persons was not "practical" was astonishing. Former home minister of a state commented on a rival candidate for assembly election who was in jail on rape charges that "at least he could have raped after the election." Incidentally, he was forced earlier to step down from the post of home minister following his remark, '*Itne bade sheher mein chhota hadsa ho jaata hai*' on the horrific 26/11 terrorist attack in Mumbai. Home minister of another state justified rape by describing it as a social crime that can be "right sometimes wrong sometimes."

Such remarks of politicians indicate a dangerous dive in their maturity levels and are not indicative of a seasoned democracy. They suffer from verbal diarrhea and seldom take responsibility for their irresponsible and undignified remarks insulting dignity of women and are made in an effort to gain cheap popularity.

Not only of politicians and religious leaders, the mindset of the rapists also regards women as men's property and rape as 'deserved punishment'. The remorseless and completely unrepentant rapists of Nirbhaya, said, "Women who go out at night have only themselves to blame if they attract the attention of gangs of male molesters" and "*yeh to sab karte hain.*" In his shocking interview to a documentary, one of the defence lawyers said, "If you keep sweets on the street then dogs will come and eat them." What all such perverted minds have is the belief that women are of lesser value. Some have remarked that use of mobile phones is responsible for crime against women, which is utterly shocking. Mobile phones, "influence of western culture" and "vulgar dressing" have been the focus of patriarchal ire and *Khap panchayats*. Such skewed views hold women as natural objects for sex.

To single out such people would be unfair, as even judges sometimes hold women of lesser value. In a 1982 judgment, judge Bertrand of Ipswich Crown Court let off a car driver of sexually assaulting a woman with a fine of 2,000 pounds on the ground that the woman was also guilty of "contributory negligence" for request for lift at night. Again, in June 2007, another British judge, Julian Hall of Oxford County Court, awarded a lenient nine-month prison to a rapist since the 10-year old victim "liked to dress provocatively" and looked as if she was 16. In India, the Supreme Court acquitted two policemen of rape charges in 1978 on the ground that the 16-year old girl did not raise any alarm while being sexually assaulted inside the police station and on the ground that the behaviour of the girl suggested that she was habituated to sexual intercourse. However, SC has changed its approach and observed in one of the cases in 1991 that a woman is "equally entitled to protection of law. Therefore, merely because she is of easy virtue, her evidence cannot be thrown out."

Provocative, disrespectful and insulting statements, and irresponsible remarks are not only reserved for rape victims but also made by politicians in the Parliament and on many other platforms in other contexts also. Vile, abusive and unparliamentary language spewed by prominent political players is unacceptable in any democracy and should not be permitted in the Parliament or in public. Characterisation and shameful remarks damaging the dignity of an individual has now become a common habit of most leaders and no party is immune to it. Fearing public backlash, the irresponsible remarks are either denied by them later on or given a different meaning to satisfy the press or the people. Even though denied or withdrawn, they dent the secular and social character of the nation and do more harm than any good to the country and the government.

It is a blessing of democracy that every person can freely express his views and the downside is that this torrent of words gets immediately into circulation with both positive and negative results leading to social reaction. Due to this malaise our democracy has become a barren landscape of brittle mediocrity, and indiscriminate, casual or irresponsible remarks cause political storms and contribute to divisive tendencies. There must be a Line of Speech Control for our leaders and repeated crossing of '*Laxman Rekha*' should be a punishable offence and should not be permitted under Freedom of Speech. Legislators deserve to be censured by the Parliament for their undignified and unparliamentary remarks and there should not be different standards for commoners and MPs.

In all patriarchal societies, such as ours, women are often the most vulnerable. Gender discrimination is strongly embedded in our social class for centuries that has also led to disrespect to women. Increasing violence against women and children needs to be confronted and curtailed by government action and strict enforcement of law. Police and judicial reforms are perhaps more important than economic reforms today if we are to lay claim to being a civilised and progressive democratic society. Unfortunately, we do not have the social and political will to root out discrimination against women which is also reflected in the sex ratio and child mortality ratio. Number of females in comparison to males has been declining. According to 2011 census it was 940 females per 1000 males.

Our education system also appears to have failed to impart the values of equality, resulting in disrespect for women. Constitution guarantees equal rights to all citizens but in practice some cultures in India disempowered women in matters of marriage, divorce, rights over children and inheritance. *'Beti Bachao, Beti Padhao'* is a laudable scheme of the government for women empowerment. Pranab Mukherjee also said, "Only a nation that respects and empowers its women can become a global power." Gender equality is paramount for a successful democracy for a one wing sparrow cannot fly. We dream emergence of an India that is more humane, progressive, self-confident and one envisaged by the founding fathers of our republic.

Besides women, another section of Indian society that has been widely neglected and discriminated against is of lesbian, gay, bisexual and transgender (LGBT), binary notion of gender (male or female). They reflect in Indian Penal Code and also in laws relating to divorce, inheritance, succession and other welfare institutions. In 2009, Delhi high court suggested amendment to Section 377 of the IPC as it infringed Article 15(1) of the Constitution. On December 11, 2013, SC set aside the judgment and upheld the validity of Section 377, which made consensual sex between gay adults, even in private, a 'crime' which would attract a maximum punishment of life imprisonment saying that a person's carnal preference had to be only heterosexual.

Decision of the Supreme Court was a cruel blow to the aspirations of lakhs of homosexuals and drew outrage of international media. All India Muslim Personal Law Board, RSS and some church bodies considered homosexuality a sin and were against 'carnal' and 'unnatural sex'. Liberal promoters on sexual choice lay more stress on universal human rights and scientific evidence. There is a fundamental conflict between communities that abhor same-sex relationships and the right of gays to live by their own morals. For everything that is true in India, the opposite turns out to be equally true.

In a historic judgment in September, 2018, a bench of five judges of the Honourable Supreme Court unanimously held the 2013 ruling arbitrary and legalised consensual sexual relations among gay adults by partially striking down Section 377. This ushered in a new dawn for the inclusive society.

Regarding transgender and endocrinologists, psychologists and surgeons are united in their opinion that there can be no single definition for them, as the condition could be a result of biological, hormonal, genetic, psychological, environmental, or just a delusional factor. Changes in an embryonic stage can leave someone with ambiguous genitalia. Similarly, abnormalities in the adrenal gland can make a biological female develop male genitalia. Indian mythology shows that we were a much inclusive society when it comes to transgender but a couple of centuries ago we lost it due to foreign influence.

Non-recognition of the identity of *hijras*/transgenders in various legislations denied them equal protection of law. In a landmark verdict SC declared that government cannot deprive a person his/her legal right to acquire preferred gender through sex change operation. The judgment deserves appreciation in providing recognition to transgenders as 'third gender' and including them among 'Other Backward Class' (OBC) communities to avail 27% reservation in government educational institutions. This is a great leap towards social equality and will end centuries of oppression, discrimination and insult suffered by transgenders.

Gay, lesbians and other members of the rainbow community find prominent place among the great people in the world. Alan Turing who cracked the impossible cryptic Nazi code that helped victory in Second World War, was judicially sentenced to forced chemical castration because he was gay. He committed suicide. Again, Tim Cook, the boss of Apple, Newton, the great scientist, Eric Allman, the man who invented the modern internet, Tchaikovsky, Byron, Auden, Wittgenstein, Barthes, Foucault, Cole Porter, Ann Bancroft, Joan Baez, James Ivory, Navratilova, and Ralph Waldo Emerson were all gay and lesbians.

A formidable social force that has forced the government to change rape laws and has championed the cause of LGBT is the Indian middle class. This class, hitherto dismissed as an insignificant segment of the electorate, is fast emerging as a mighty social force. On the basis of monthly income between rupees 20,000 and rupees 1,00,000 the size of the middle class has grown from paltry 25 million in 1996 to over 267 million in 2015. It is more homogenious with strong common interests and aspirations. Though not entirely free from narrower regional or local considerations, the marginalised educated urban middle class is frustrated by India's vote-bank politics and believe less in "folk theory" that prefers voting on the basis of caste, community, race, peer and other special interest groups. The class has instant connectivity through mobile and internet and is an avid user of social media and television.

The first formidable sign of middle-class unity was visible in Jessica Lal case when Manu Sharma who had killed her in 1999 in front of dozens of witnesses, was acquitted. The middle class publicly displayed its anger through candle light vigils and other public displays, leading to the reversal of the verdict. Again, the same nation-wide mobilisation was visible during Anna Hazare's anti-corruption '*satyagraha*' in 2011 and the 'Nirbhaya' gang-rape case braving water cannons, shouting slogans, holding protest marches and courting arrest across the country. The potential political entity is still disorganised and has no strong leadership. Its anger on lack of governance, corruption, unemployment and women-safety is demanding answer to ill-advised policies. They normally favour order, stability and identify themselves with issues and not social groups. They are exponents of independent thought and not partisan loyalty. The growing reality is that they want clean and efficient government and sometimes defy all theories of sociologists. Their protests have awakened people and may not stop until they achieve their goal. Emergence of middle-class intelligentsia is the hope to protect democracy, the dumb dame, from constant and brutal rape by politicians, bureaucrats, and even legislature.

Middle class with all its knowledge and strength is a formidable force to change the course of elections through the power of its franchise. Social scientists who analyse events like elections on the basis of their own set theories and social engineers who form fomulas and equations for predicting election results are sometimes baffled by the way the voters theories about events. They often fail to read their minds and social side of the events. In politics, parties winning massive mandates may be decimated next. Factors like luck and chance often determine the fate of elections as much as the price of onions. Predictable factor of caste also sometimes fails and anti-incumbency has swallowed many established governments while good governments have been rewarded with pro-incumbency also. Despite years of experience in politics and films, you never know what your audience is thinking. Political parties must shun traditional media and take recourse to social media to reach young voters. Dividing voters along old fault lines was once as easy as parting one's hair, but not any longer. The established parties blindly ride the crest of a wave but do not realise that over time waves recede leaving behind nothing but marsh.

Emergence of middle class is also reinforcing the Right wing leading to strengthening of democratic institutions. After independence Indian democracy had swayed to Left due to the policies of Congress resulting in a disturbing decline in independent right-wing intellectuals. Indian university campuses, nurseries of political thought, have also been dominated by the Left. Politics today is brutally competitive and it is becoming difficult for intellectuals to survive in it as it is a business of money and muscle. Significant example is of scholar PM Manmohan Singh who could never win a Lok Sabha seat. With the Election Commission deciding to confer voting rights on NRIs, electoral battles will soon be fought on a global canvas strengthening the Right Wing.

Emergence of middle class is leading to gradual fading out of old political leaders giving way to younger ones. Many of these younger leaders are rejecting identity politics and opting for development-based and issue-based policies. Once this churning process reaches its logical culmination, it might lead to a new equilibrium. The danger, however, is youthful impatience that may give rise to frustration of the middle class due to absence of strong and pragmatic leadership, economic development and adequate job opportunities. The class wants immediate results and does not realise that 'Rome was not built in a day'.

Change is a mist which floats through events. A visible shift is taking place in the structure of party politics and in the behaviour of the electorate due to improvement in economic fortunes. With prosperity has also come empowerment. Economic and social issues now matter far more and caste, community and religious affiliation is losing ground. Today, the voter is not lured by monetary inducements but wants the governments to deliver good governance and to move beyond narrow sectarian identities of caste and religion. Regarding the aspirations of the youth, APJ Abdul Kalam, said, "…the youth want democracy to be re-invented with faster growth." Democracy can only be strengthened by introducing socio-economic reforms more vigorously, strengthening political institutions, controlling corruption, and enforcing rule of law without fear or favour.

13

NARROW WINDING PATH

The word 'caste' is derived from Portuguese/Spanish '*casta*' meaning breed or race. Contrary to the claim of some, the present caste system in India was not sanctified by our ancient scriptures. BR Ambedkar, in his scholarly book 'Who were the *Shudras*?', had proved from texts and scriptures that in ancient times, India had widely respected '*Shudra*' rulers as well, and a caste system based on birth was interpolated into the texts later. In Bhagwat Gita, Lord Krishna enunciates that He created the four '*vernas*' based on '*guna*' (attributes) and '*karma*', and not on birth. General consensus among historians and anthropologists is that caste rigidity and discrimination emerged in the Smriti period, after the birth of Christ. Caste system was challenged in the medieval period by '*bhakti*' movement and powerful empires like Kakatiyas led by '*Shudra*' rulers emerged. Birth-based caste system became rigid around the British rule and has remained so since then.

During the colonial rule, India was viewed by the British through the lens of categories rather than the people. They classified historically disadvantaged sections in India's rigid caste hierarchy as depressed classes. In the August 4, 1932 Communal Awards, they extended their proposal of separate electorates for Muslims, Christians, etc. to the depressed classes. This was a sinister ploy of 'divide-and-rule'. The first listing (scheduling) of these castes started for 1937 elections and was extended after independence when no effort was made to create a casteless society.

Indian Constitution abolished untouchability but provided reservation to Scheduled Castes (SC) and Scheduled Tribes (ST) to the extent of 15% and 7.5% respectively. The attempt was to address and eliminate horrific discrimination suffered by low castes and to slowly assimilate the historically oppressed in social mainstream. Rationale for reservations was to allow SCs and STs to acquire education and socially viable skills that would give them dignity and bring them into the mainstream of society. Caste reservations introduced at that time were considered to be a temporary phase for eradication of inequality. Sadly, they not only continued but even expanded with more and more castes demanding reservation and political parties liberally agreeing for their vote-bank.

Institution of caste is central to the undemocratic character of Indian life. Ambedkar also viewed castes as anti-national that bring about separation in social life, generate jealousy and antipathy between castes. This destroys fraternity and "fraternity can be a fact only when there is a nation. Without fraternity, equality and liberty will be no deeper than coats of paint." He was open to the idea of revisiting some aspects of reservation and to make it an interim measure for social justice but beneficiaries have expanded demanding special treatment in different sectors. The constitutional aspiration was to create a society that could transcend caste but the trajectory that reservations have taken turned it upside down. Reservations have been grabbed by the affluent in the respective castes and have continued for generations. It has not filtered down to the poor in these castes and they continue to suffer, thus further widening inequality. There is need to cap reservation benefits as the cream in the creamy layer is only going to get thicker, denying benefits to the truly needy. By witnessing today's permanent and expanding regime of caste quotas Ambedkar would be turning over in his grave.

Unfortunately, instead of achieving the goal of wiping out caste system from our social life, we have further widened its scope during the last 70 years. In 1979, the Janta Party government under Prime Minister Morarji Desai established Mandal Commission headed by BP Mandal, a member of the Parliament, with a mandate to "identify the socially or educationally backward" and to consider the question of seat reservation and quotas to redeem caste discrimination. On the basis of eleven social, economic and educational indicators to determine backwardness, the Commission estimated that 54% of total population, excluding SCs and STs, belonging to 3743 different castes and communities were backward which has now increased to 5013 with proposal of 110 more castes for national OBC status pending with the Centre. The Commission recommended that 27% of jobs in government service and public sector undertakings be reserved for candidates belonging to "backward castes" thus bringing the total reserved category to 49.5%. In his zeal to project himself as champion of the downtrodden, VP Singh sought to implement the recommendations and they came into force on August 13, 1990 amid widespread violence and immolations.

Mandal Commission vastly expanded the ambit of reservations and made "quota" a way of life. While Ambedkar was clear that his final aim was to uproot this unjust hierarchical order from public life, Mandal had no such ambitions. Ambedkar wanted SC/ST reservations to be periodically reviewed but Mandal showed no sensitivity on this matter. While SCs and STs have no assets anywhere, OBCs do have in rural India, both in terms of land and power. They are far from being down-trodden and have been supported by political parties for their vote-bank aspirations. Powerful castes and rural dominants are now jumping the queue and demanding a share of the pie in jobs. The tragedy is that "forwards among the backwards" are cornering the 27% Mandal quota because the "backwards among the backwards" are unable to compete with them owing to their inferior educational and financial status. This has prevented social justice from filtering down and has defeated the constitutionally intended philosophy of reservation. 'Politicisation of castes' and 'casteism of politics' has weakened the functioning of our democratic system.

Extreme politicisation of caste has given rise to what may be called the politics of 'competitive backwardness', with more and more sections of the polity claiming OBC status. Now another lot called Extremely Backward Castes (EBCs) have cropped up. The weak-kneed political class has always caved into such unreasonable demands, fearing their wrath in elections. The fault lines are expanding and it now seems impossible to erase the policy of reservations.

Section 11(1) of National Commission of Backward Classes Act says that the government should, every ten years, purge the OBC list of communities that have ceased to be backward but it has not happened even once. On the other hand, reservation is being hijacked by more dominant castes. As unemployment affects everyone, all communities are trying to run wild. Patidar Patels in Gujarat, Jats in Haryana, Gujjars in Rajasthan, Kapus in Andhra Pradesh, Marathas in Maharashtra and Ahoms in Assam are powerful communities but demanding reservations. They resort to violent agitations for getting OBC status. Even though caste is distinct from religion, minorities are also demanding reservation quota. These reservations have been termed as "war of the crumbs" and if everyone gets reservation then no one gets reservation.

Supreme Court ruled in a judgment in 2015 that caste can no longer be the sole criterion of social justice and reservations. Creamy layer was defined which could not usurp reservation quota at the cost of more deserving. As a pre-poll surgical strike, Modi government passed the 10% quota bill for 'Poor Upper Castes' in January 2019 for reservation in central jobs and all educational institutions. A vibrant economy can only help in mitigating caste discrimination and disgruntled young men agitating for reservations.

Equality is one of the cardinal principles of our Constitution. Instead of bringing in equality, caste politics is widening inequality in the social and economic structure. Reservation, which was to become a ladder to climb up to reach the platform of social equality, is being used by some upper castes to climb down and claim 'backward' tag to grab a share in the reservation cake. Supreme Court had warned in 2008 against the recent trend of 'forward' castes seeking 'backward' status as such a trend stagnates the country. It said, "While affirmative discrimination is a road to equality, care should be taken that the road does not become a rut in which the vehicle of progress gets entrenched and stuck." There have been no fruitful efforts on the part of politicians to erase caste system and instead it is being nourished more and more for political interests, creating further divisions in the society. Village *Panchayats*, considered by Ambedkar as hidebound by caste, dens of inequality and cesspools of communalism, have also failed to instill the spirit of democracy among the rural masses.

It is unfortunate that our social and political leaders fail to realise that efforts should be made to make India a vibrant democracy where equality and not caste rules. Social scientists must strive to evolve a policy mechanism that would bring about a caste-less egalitarian society where equal opportunities would be an unqualified fundamental right. Reservation is a social evil and promoting it highlights a bankruptcy of ideas that gives rise to inequality and puts democracy on the path of no progress. Caste politics constricts democracy; communal politics endangers democracy.

Obsession with continuation and expansion of reservation has generated deeper social divisions. India needs freezing or rolling back caste-based reservations, focusing instead on meritocracy, quality of education and job creation. We must have a reservation policy that best achieves the primary objective of eradicating inequality rather than continue benefits to the creamy layer. Instead of creating opportunity, it simply takes opportunity from someone deserving and hands it to another, purely on the basis of birth. In doing so it divides society, fosters mediocrity and demotivates the more talented. Fairness can't be created by doing something unfair. Reservations are not the answer to social justice, education and job growth are. Inequality, lack of infrastructure and education-deficiencies are key weaknesses. To be fair to those who have been deprived so far, the creamy layer must be separated. It is said that in democracy in order to take one step forward it is often necessary to take a couple of steps sideways. China took a Great Leap Forward and India is trying to take a Great Leap Backward.

Besides caste, secularism is another most abused concept in Indian politics today. In the western definition of secularism, French Revolution separated church from state and communism erased religion from political and social life. Indian secularism is very different and believes in equality of all faiths. Persons like Swami Vivekanand wanted people to aspire to the greater virtue of acceptance of all religions rather than be content with the virtue of merely tolerating others. He said that if you were born a Hindu, be a good Hindu; if born a Muslim, be a good Muslim, and that would make both good Indians. Gandhi believed in the merger of all streams of faith stipulating uncompromised tolerance and respect for all religions and faiths. He urged that the Gita should be read with the eye of a Hindu and the Quran with the eye of a Muslim. He also said that true strength lay in faith equality and not faith supremacy. Religious customs, traditions and objects held sacred by a religion should be respected by all as respected by its followers. In a judgment Supreme Court stated that Hinduism "incorporates all forms of belief without mandating the selection or elimination of any one single belief." Hinduism has no single founder or scripture or 'truth' to uphold but is an eclectic body of realisations. Its open-ended character makes it uniquely suited to peace and stability of modern world. Upholding the liberal and pluralist character of Hinduism will preserve both the essence of religion and integrity of India. Pranab Mukherjee said, "Our national identity has emerged after a long-drawn process of confluence and assimilation…The soul of India lies in pluralism and tolerance. Secularism and inclusion is a matter of faith for us." History has affirmed that pluralism is inevitable in India.

The simplest description of secularism is letting all religions coexist; coexist like milk and sugar and not like oil and water. India has evolved over millennia in a way that religion and its practices have been left out of the domain of the state. In a landmark ruling, the Bombay High Court said that no government body can compel an individual to declare his or her religion. Religious minorities need protection against discrimination and extra help to overcome their social and economic backwardness but secularism should not lead to appeasement of minorities. Appeasement of minorities is actually ghettoisation of minorities through a carrot-and-stick strategy allied with fear of majority backlash. Prosperity of minority communities and of democracy is complimentary to each other. Minority communities must be encouraged to assimilate with the majority community without abandoning their own culture. Their success lies on education, liberal values and more modern and open-minded approach to religion. They cannot progress if they fall easy prey to polarisation and illusionary appeasements.

Whereas secularism in the West is absence of religion, in India it is pluri-religiousness and is integral to nationalism. True secularism means a strict separation of religion from state and political administration. To check the tendency of political parties to exploit the voters, the Supreme Court in its judgment in January 2017 widened the scope of Section 123(3) of The Representation of the People Act which prohibited the seeking of votes in the name of religion, caste, race, community or language.

Today, secularism of politicians is more opportunistic and instead of equality of all faiths it shifts to dualism. Secularism today is secularism of convenience and changes from religion to religion and person to person. What is secular for one becomes non-secular for the other. Some parties are exploiting 'secularism' for vote-bank and putting the future of democracy in grave danger. India is the only country in the world where dawn is preceded by '*aazan*', and followed by the music of temple bells, reciting of Guru Granth Sahib and pealing of church bells. Faith-equality is the basis of civilised political and social stability, for otherwise rage takes the shape of outrage.

In Indian Constitution, Article 44 of Directive Principles of state policy mandates that "the state shall endeavour to secure for all citizens a Uniform Civil Code throughout the territory of India." Hindu law was codified but question of common code towards reform of Muslim personal laws was sidestepped. It was mainly on account of the stubbornness of Nehru that UCC did not become a part of the Constitution and became a part of Directive Principles. He said that UCC had his "extreme sympathy" but the time was not "ripe" for it. Nehru did not push it even later and Ambedkar, the first law minister, quit the Cabinet in utter disgust in 1951. He said, "I have never seen a case of a child whip so disloyal to the Prime Minister and the Prime Minister so loyal to the disloyal whip." It was a grave blunder on the part of Nehru not to reinforce the idea of an egalitarian democratic society. He lacked the political courage and the golden opportunity was lost. Successive governments did not intervene in the domain of Muslim personal laws mainly due to vote-bank politics.

Staunch supporters of UCC argue that secular citizenship means strict equality before law, and that India's regime of distinct personal laws, which discriminate against women, should be replaced by a fair civil code. They also hold that existence of religious and personal laws had kept the nation divided into watertight compartments. For unity of the nation they propagete "One nation, one Constitution, one law" theory. Those who resist UCC argue that a secular state implied religious freedom for citizens of different communities to follow their personal law and this would advance national unity. They also say that secularism is not a one-size-fit-all models, and that instead of uniform laws, the state should push for uniform principles of gender justice and individual freedom. The pitfall created in the beginning in the path of Indian democracy has still not been made smooth and may not be possible in near future due to short-sightedness of one person.

No modern liberal democracy has separate personal laws based on religion. The Supreme Court has held that Muslim women are at disadvantage under the Muslim Personal Law with no safeguard against arbitrary divorce and polygamy, and this violated their fundamental right. They also held that marriage and succession are not part of religion and the Muslim Personal Law has to evolve with the changing times. The court also said that practice of polygamy is injurious to public morals and can be banned just like the practice of '*sati*' was banned. Markandey Katju, former Supreme Court judge, also said, "The Muslim personal law is barbaric, backward and unjust…it is a feudal law." All political parties have now politicised the issue to divide the society on the lines of caste and religion as a source of vote-bank.

The real battle is between liberals and conservatives, and between male chauvinists and women's rights champions. Conservatives lay more stress on divine sanction and unconditional obedience to religious commandments and this makes social reforms with changing times difficult. Same is the case with '*talaq*', divorce initiated by husband. Out of three types of '*talaqs*', '*talaq-e-biddat*', or instant divorce is three times saying '*talaq*' without any '*iddat*' period. In a 3-2 majority verdict, Supreme Court struck down on August 22, 2017 the 1,400-year old controversial *Shariat*-dictated Islamic practice of instant '*talaq*', terming it unconstitutional, arbitrary and whimsical mode of ending marriage that violated Muslim women's fundamental right to equality. It upheld the supremacy of Constitution at the altar of religion. It also remarked that law shouldn't recognise dictates of personal law in civil and family matters like divorce, marriage and adoption. The judgment spells a dawn of freedom for Muslim women and relieves them of the injustice done to them in unilateral termination of matrimonial relationship. India now joins many other Muslim countries in striking down this arbitrary practice of instantaneous '*talaq*'.

Diversity in India is at the core of all social problems. In Goa, Hindus are still governed by the Portuguese family and succession laws, and limited polygamy is permissible for them. The *Shariat* Act of 1937 is not applicable to Jammu & Kashmir. Asking for 'One nation, one law' is deeply difficult. Justice is a work in progress rather than a stable reality. One way out is that the believers may keep their customs, but if any dispute arises and the matter comes to the court, those disputes should be settled by the Indian civil code as envisaged by the Constitution. This will ensure not only full freedom of religion to the individual but also fulfill the constitutional goal of a Uniform Civil Code. Nothing is perfect in the world and in pursuit of 'best' we should not sacrifice 'good'. The best is to choose less worse.

Religion and democracy have always been at variance with each other. Whereas religion is a matter of individual faith, not prone to change, democracy is a social faith prone to change with times for the welfare of society. Religion comes from God and its purpose is to unite and not divide. Gandhiji said, "Religion is a force for unity; we cannot make it a cause of conflict." Hindu philosophy believes in *Ekam satya, bipraha bahuda vedanti*: The truth is one, the wise call it by different names. Today, intolerance and absence of social cohesion are due to intellectual shallowness, and relations between communities and regions are not free of wrinkles.

In the land where all religions have peacefully flourished, exploitation on the basis of religion started with the 'divide-and-rule' policy of the colonial rulers and has continued due to vote-bank politics. One of the consequences of religious intolerance which is not only inter-religious but intra-religious also, is communal riots that bleed the country and continue to recur every now and then. The worst took place in Gujarat in 1969 and Justice Jagmohan Reddy Commission indicted the partisan role of police. Recommendations of Justice DP Madon Commission on Bhiwandi, Jalgaon and Madad riots of 1970, Justice Josepth Vithyathil Commision on Tellicherry riots of 1971, Justice Ranganath Misra Commission report on 1984-riots in Delhi and report of National Human Rights Commission on the 2002 Gujarat riots, have all remained unimplemented. Communal killings in Muzaffarnagar in 20014 and the ethnic cleansing of Pandits from Kashmir became the theatre of deadly dance of communal riots. Such incidents tarnish the fair name of Indian democracy that takes pride in its pluralistic society. Committees and commissions are appointed but reports and action is waited for years. Short public memory soon fades away and mind gets ready to receive news of yet another carnage. In the past, riots only happened in cities, but now the country side is also not free of ethnic disturbances. The mute mud walls are still standing but everything within has changed.

Fundamentalism is a deadly poison that easily ignites sparks of communal hatred and violence. It brings the worst in man in volatile times and threatens the democratic, pluralistic and secular values. It is hard to reason with emotionally charged people for whom emotions matter more than reason, or even truth. Religious intolerance is the greatest danger to the survival of democracy in India and a grave threat to its disintegration. It has been there for centuries and shows no sign of easing.

Irrationality of thought, religious intolerance and absence of secularism cannot be equated with illiteracy and even the rational intelligentsia is bitten by its parasite. In April 2015, the conclave of chief justices of high courts (HCs), under the leadership of HL Dattu, Chief Justice of India, began on Friday, 'Good Friday', to discuss, debate and find solutions to the problems ailing judiciary. A Supreme Court judge, Kurian Joseph, not otherwise required to attend the conclave, wrote to the CJI questioning the choice of Good Friday, a day of religious significance for Christians, for the conclave. Such conclaves had been held on religious occasions in the past also. Two other Christian judges attended the conclave. Another recent example is of a disgruntled intellectual herd retired from very dignified constitutional and bureaucratic posts trying to make blatant attempts to rekindle religious sentiments to divide India. Their aim is to create intolerance among the minorities to gain cheap popularity and favour of local and foreign media. Such intellectual idiocy simply dilutes the strength of Indian democracy.

In India, we have always attempted to classify every decision either as, the will of the "authoritarian majority", "minority appeasement" "secularism" or "fundamentalism". Democratic dissent is equated with disloyalty and those in opposition are considered to be enemies. Quoting Vivekananda is being considered as *Hindutva* even though he believed deeply in the truth of all religions. Narrow-minded focus on differences; liberals explore similarities.

As institutional religions became intolerant, the disadvantaged and lower middle class were pushed towards '*deras*' which are a confluence of caste and religion. Their followers subsist on the margins both in economy and caste system and there is no caste discrimination in '*deras*'. Over the years '*deras*' have accumulated land and property worth thousands of crores and political class also exploits them to use their support-base to their advantage in polls.

'*Dera Sacha Sauda*' is a significant example of '*dera*' culture. Its chief, Gurmeet Ram Rahim, reinvented '*dera*' culture in a new market-driven economy. He began to wear flamboyant dress and jewellery, and started making money from films. Armed men freely roamed in his '*dera*' and CMs and prominent political leaders began to visit his '*dera*' regularly to tilt his massive followings for their political advantage. In 2002 he was accused of rape, sentenced to 20 years of rigorous imprisonment in August 2017 and slapped a fine of Rs 30 lakh. His followers resorted to extreme violence which led to destruction of property worth thousands of crores and loss of life of 38 people. Punjab and Haryana high court indicted the BJP government and said, "It was a political surrender just to allure the vote-bank."

Gurmeet Ram Rahim is not the only self-styled godman charged of unlawful activities. Asaram had built an empire of ten thousand crores of rupees with 400 '*ashrams*' in India and abroad. He and his son Narayan Sai have also been convicted of sexual abuse. Crores were offered to the victim, witnesses were killed, judges were threatened and journalists were attacked. Blind faith blindfolds even rich and educated and some in high government positions supported him saying that the case had been framed against him.

There are many other self-styled godmen who have fallen foul of the law. Some of the prominent ones are, Nityananda, head of Dhyanpeeth Charitable Trust, Shiv Murty Dwivedi or Ichchadhari Baba who re-invented himself as Swami Bhimanand, Rampal founder of Satlok Ashram at Hisar, Anand Murty, Virendra Dev Dikshit, Ram Vriksh Yadav, Ashutosh Maharaj, Swami Vikasanad and Balak Brahmchari. All such institutions of blind faith weaken democracy and encourage forces of caste and religious discrimination.

Existence of democracy is under constant threat all over the world and terrorism is its most heinous menace. A 'culture of offendedness' and hatred, has given rise to the virus of terrorism that selects its victims without any apparent reason. Main aim of the terrorists is to annihilate secular forces, spread anarchy and wipe out democracy from the world. As many as 87 countries experienced a terrorist incident in 2013. Globally, four terrorist groups - al-Qaida, Boko Haram, ISIS and Taliban - were responsible for 66% of all deaths from terrorist attacks in 2013.

Besides religious fanaticism, the root cause of terrorism is poverty and unemployment that drives young men to become *'jihadi'* foot soldiers. They have no religion, adhere to no ideology and become soft targets for brainwashing. India has become a victim of vicious cross-border terrorism. Repeated ceasefire violations need "incisive diplomacy and impregnable security mechanism". In the 1993 Mumbai terrorist bomb attack, mastered by our volatile neighbourhood, 257 people died and 713 were injured. In 2022, 38 people were sentenced to death for widespread bomb attacks in Ahmedabad city of Gujarat in 2008 that had left 56 people dead.

According to the Global Terrorism Index 2014, India was the sixth worst-affected country by terrorism in 2013 and deaths from terrorism increased by 70%. In India as many as 43 different terrorist groups were found to be operational which were categorised into three groups: Islamist, separatists and communists. Communist terrorist groups are by far the most frequent perpetrators in India. Police are the main target of Maoists, accounting for half of all deaths and injuries. Economic disparities are politicised for ulterior political motives that also gives rise to militant movements. India needs a strong, decisive and far-sighted leader to solve the Naxalite and Maoist issue.

World powers need comprehensive and sustained effort to strike hard wherever terror raises its monstrous head but they are soft due to their greed of expansionism and for geopolitical competition over the control of natural resources in the regions of conflict. Due to their divided policies on terrorism some strong terrorist group may sustain sovereignty over a country and then spread its tentacles by becoming a legal terrorist power. The only way to contain the new international instability is to search for solutions on the basis of dialogue, dignity and respect for international law. It must also be kept in mind that terrorism wants to be attacked and it gains, rather than loses as a result of our attempts to tame it. Cutting economic supply lines and providing dignified and gainful employment for their recruits are the solutions. According to a US intelligence report "current Islamist phase of terrorism" might end by 2030 but might evolve into bloodless forms of economic and financial terrorism. A world where humiliation reigns will remain torn by terrorism, conflicts and crisis that will be grave dangers for the survival of democracy.

International forces and those aided and encouraged by them within the country are trying to disintegrate India in order to deprive it becoming a vibrant economy. On the eve of his Independence Day address on 14th August 2015 Pranab Mukherjee said that there were challenges to India's pluralist, tolerant and patient culture. Vested interests chip away at social harmony in an attempt to erode many centuries of secularism. He also stressed that "pluralism and tolerance have held together for ages this civilisation of many languages, races, religions, with diverse anthropological features." The light of liberalism opens the minds and radiates tolerance. Caucasian, Dravidian and Mongoloid ethnic groups speak 122 languages and 1600 dialects, and profess seven faiths. They have all survived and thrived mainly due to the tolerance of Hinduism. In a SC judgment it was observed, "Hinduism is a tolerant faith, which has enabled Islam, Christianity, Zoroastrianism, Judaism, Buddhism, Jainism and Sikhism to find shelter and support upon this land." It is now for these religions to reciprocate tolerance and make India a vibrant democracy.

India prides in its pluralistic ideas where many religions have thrived due to its assimilative capacity. No other nation exists with as much diversity of language, ethnic identity and religions with 1.3 billion people. Democracy in India and also all over the world is under constant stress and threat of collapse. Globally people are getting dissatisfied the way democracy is functioning due to inefficiency, inability to manage crisis, and brute forces of mobocracy. In India the danger is due to religious and intellectual intolerance. Tolerant democracy is the only way forward if India were to progress and be a proud global nation.

14

LEVELING PITS AND BUMPS

India's claim to largest democracy rests on the strength of three pillars - legislature, executive and judiciary - besides media, the fourth one. Independence of judiciary and rule of law are the backbone of every democracy and if law fails, democracy derails. Efficiency of a judicial system depends on the efficiency of courts and that of the police system which helps the judicial system in the investigation of crimes for speedy delivery of justice. Judiciary and police are thus two vital organs for maintaining 'rule of law' and strengthening democracy.

Indian Constitution bestowed the executive with the power to appoint judges of Supreme Court and high courts in "consultation" with the Chief Justice of India (CJI). In all these appointments executive had primacy and role of judiciary was advisory/consultative. BR Ambedkar clarified that consultation with the CJI should not be viewed as requiring his concurrence since that would give him a veto over appointments. This system of appointment of judges continued till 1981.

The intrusion of executive in the appointment of judges gave rise to "committed judiciary" from the time of Indira Gandhi as PM. In 1993, SC ruled that primacy in appointing judges vested with judiciary and a 9-judge bench by majority of seven, ruled that CJI would appoint judges, reducing the executive to mere rubber stamp. In 1998, on presidential reference, a 9-judge bench reaffirmed the 1993 judgment. Spate of corruption scandals left the political class with little will and moral authority to protest against the judiciary's move. The system of appointing judges to SC and HCs, popularly referred to as 'judges appointing judges scheme', is known as the 'collegiums system'.

The second Administrative Reforms Commission report stated bluntly, "In no other country in the world does the judiciary appoint itself." Judicial Public Service Commission like UPSC, manned by retired senior judges was suggested for appointment of judges. Increase of corruption cases in judiciary was also a matter of grave concern for the government. CJI VN Khare candidly admitted that corruption in judiciary was rampant. In 2011, 75 complaints of corruption against serving judges of SC and HCs were sent to CJI or CJs of the respective high courts for "appropriate action" but not aware if any action was taken. For accountability and to check corruption, judiciary should have a Lokpal for itself which will act as a watchdog with investigative and prosecution powers. Process of removal of judges of the higher judiciary is very cumbersome and they can be removed only by impeachment that requires parliamentary endorsement and no judge has been impeached so far.

Besides corruption in judiciary, two instances within the higher judiciary are shocking. Justice CS Karnan was notorious for his self-styled orders and frequently leveled capricious charges against other judges who were his colleagues. As a judge of Madras high court, he precipitated crisis by passing strictures against its then Chief Justice, stayed his own transfer order to the Calcutta high court and passed 'orders' imprisoning CJI and seven other judges of the Supreme Court. In an unprecedented order by a 7-judge SC bench he was sentenced to six months imprisonment in May 2017. He argued that he was being victimised since he was a Dalit.

In another classic case the Supreme Court was thrown into its biggest-ever crisis on January 12, 2017 when its four senior-most judges launched an astonishing public attack against the CJI for his allegedly arbitrary way of assigning important cases to benches headed by junior SC judges ignoring senior ones. They held a press-meet on the lawns of the bungalow of Justice J Chelameswar. It gave "hawkish politicians" a "handle to interfere" in judiciary affairs. Parliament unanimously passed a law to set up a National Judicial Appointments Commission (NJAC) to broaden the process of recruiting members of higher judiciary which was struck down by the Supreme Court.

Appointments, earlier by the executive and from 1998 by the collegiums have been widely criticised. In July 1994, Justice Markandey Katju made the revelation that a 'tainted' judge of a high court was confirmed in his post owing to political pressure exerted on former PM Manmohan Singh by DMK, Tamil Nadu ally of the coalition. DMK had also threatened to pull out of the government on issues of Tamilians in Sri Lanka, allotment of portfolios, and disinvestment in Neyveli Lignite Corporation. Elevation of Justice PD Dinakaran to SC in 2010 also sparked a public debate on the subject of corruption in the appointment of judges.

The subject of judicial appointments has been a see-saw battle between executive and judiciary. The process of replacing the collegiums with a panel was initiated by NDA government in 2003 but the bill was never taken up by Parliament. In 2014 UPA government again initiated the NJAC to replace the collegiums system. Both Houses of the Parliament unanimously passed National Judicial Appointments Commission Act which was ratified by 20 states as is mandatory for a constitutional amendment bill. On October 16, 2015, a five-judge bench of Supreme Court, by a 4-1 majority, declared the 99th constitutional amendment as "unconstitutional and void" on the ground that the inclusion of a politician (law minister) and two eminent persons as members who could join hands was fraught with danger of serious interference with judicial independence. A minister influencing the judiciary can be judged from an incident quoted by a former Union law minister HR Bhardwaj. He was "under tremendous pressure from Manmohan Singh government" to get a favourable order from Supreme Court on UPA's decision to impose President's rule in Bihar in 2005 to prevent JD(U)-BJP combine from coming to power. Bhardwaj said that he even met the then Chief Justice YK Sabharwal but "could not summon the nerves to broach the topic" even though he was his family friend.

Supreme Court admitted that "all is not well" with collegiums system. The system has proven itself vulnerable to graft and nepotism. In one of the cases, the Supreme Court had observed, "Judges should be stern stuff and tough fire, unbending before power, economic or political, and they must uphold the core principle of rule of law which says 'be you ever so high, the law is above you'." A number of qualities like integrity, intellectual capacity, a sound knowledge of law, good temper, judicial approach to matters to be decided and a good health may have to be considered but, as Winston Churchill said, these qualities were not to be measured in terms of pounds, shillings and pence. Ex-chief justice of the US Supreme Court, John Marshal said that the judiciary's power lies not in deciding cases nor in imposing sentences nor in punishing for contempt, but in the trust, confidence and faith of the common man.

The Constitution makers had ensured that three organs of government, legislature, executive and judiciary must have mutual respect for each other and work in their respective spheres without disturbing the balance of powers. Unbridled executive interference has always been dangerous but judicial activism should also not lead to dilution of the separation of powers. The function of judiciary is to interpret laws and not make them but judiciary is often blamed for over-reaching into legislative and executive domains upsetting the equilibrium. Similarly, the executive's failures and lack of accountability have often led people to approach the judiciary for justice. For the smooth functioning of democracy all branches of government must stay within established boundaries and raise their bar of efficiency.

Justice is reflective of quality of democracy, and a fair and speedy justice-delivery system is of paramount importance for its survival. The wheels of justice, the saying goes, grind slowly but grind exceedingly fine. 'Justice delayed is justice denied' and also 'Justice delayed is injustice perpetrated'. Delay in trial encourages crime to thrive and the corrupt to dig deep into the system with impunity.

Some of the cases of delayed justice are really startling. Wrongly accused of pocketing rupees 57.60 out of money-order distribution, a postman was proved innocent after 29 years. In another bizarre instance, a bus conductor of Delhi Transport Corporation, which suffers a loss of about rupees 1,000 crore annually, was charged for negligence and cheating for charging 5 paise less on a ticket from a passenger and was dismissed. The case went on for 41 years before it was finally dismissed by the high court but the review petition is still pending. In yet another instance, a case dragged on for 54 years in a trial court in which 6 of the 10 petitioners passed away when the case finally reached its end.

A former railway minister LN Mishra succumbed to his injuries when bombs were hurled at him. After 40 years, the court convicted four Ananda Margis and an advocate on December 8, 2014. Out of the Congress leaders involved in the 1984-riots, Sajjan Kumar was convicted by Delhi high court and sentenced to jail on December 17, 2018. Justice RK Gauba lamented that the process of deciding the guilt was "reduced to the level of academic exercise." The Hon'ble Judge also observed that the failure of criminal justice administration may crumble or lose its potency is no longer a distant doomsday scenario.

In another case, the famous Bollywood actor Salman Khan, was found guilty of culpable homicide not amounting to murder after his car killed one and injured four people sleeping on a dimly lit footpath. It took 13 years to judge who was driving the car and whether or not he was under the influence of alcohol. He was sentenced to five-year imprisonment by the high court and appeal is pending in the Supreme Court. Surprisingly, a Bollywood singer reacted to the incident in a shocking way by saying, "If a dog sleeps on the road, he will die a dog's death." In another case, Navjot Singh Sidhu, a famous cricketer and Punjab Congress President, was sentenced to one-year imprisonment in a road-rage case after 33 years. Such cases take only few months in many other countries.

The other side of the picture is more startling where people convicted of heinous crimes are locked up for years before being found innocent on appeal. A person was convicted for dacoity and murder in 1982 and, on appeal, finally acquitted in 2015 due to wrongful conviction. In fairness, the state must compensate those found to have been wrongfully confined. The right to life under Article 21 of the Constitution extends to a convict's right to a speedy justice also. Justice Verma committee report stresses that "speedy justice is not merely an aspect of the right to life with dignity, but is essential for efficacy of law."

Another glaring fact is that of under-trials languishing in jails for long. In 2012, out of 3.81 lakh prisoners, 2.54 lakh were under-trials. Many of these had spent more time in jail than the sentence they would have got had they been convicted for the crime they were arrested for. Supreme Court observed in one of the judgments, "We appear to be obsessed with arresting people though there are effective ways other than arrest to bring them to justice." The Apex Court on September 5, 2014 set a deadline of two months to release all under-trial prisoners on personal bond who had served half of maximum sentence prescribed for the offences they had been charged. Illegal arrests and fake encounters are other blots on our judicial system. According to National Human Rights Commission, there were a total of 3,950 cases of illegal arrests in the country from April 2010 to July 2013. A chilling case revealed that the motive behind the fake encounter was to earn awards and recognition for killing "terrorists". All these lapses are a slur on the fair name of democracy.

It is unfortunate that the rigour of law does not apply uniformly to different strata of society. Citizens with means and power buy their way out of criminal charges. Ministers do not vacate their official residence on ceasing to be minister and convert the residence into a memorial for the departed leaders. In 70 years, we have not been able to achieve the goal to provide justice to people and create an atmosphere where everybody has equality of opportunity and status defeating the very purpose of a vibrant democracy.

Perhaps one of the biggest challenges faced by the Indian judiciary is massive burden of pending cases. As per figures of September 30, 2016, the Supreme Court had nearly 61,000 pending cases, high courts had more than 40 lakh cases and all subordinate courts together had yet to dispose of around 2.9 crore cases. In terms of time, it will take 324 years for various courts to clear the pending cases. This is besides the fresh cases that will come up during this period. There is also a substantial increase in the cases filed in the courts. Some three decades back, the number was around three per thousand people which has increased to 15. Due to spurt in crimes, and increase in literacy rate and per capita income, this is likely to increase to about 75 cases in the next three decades.

A variety of factors contribute to delay in disposal of cases including lack of court management system, frequent adjournments, strikes by lawyers, accumulation of first appeals, indiscriminate use of writ jurisdiction and lack of adequate arrangements to monitor, track and bunch cases for hearing. A pervasive reason for delays is adjournments and SC has expressed "anguish, agony and concern" over indiscriminate adjournments. Fines on lower court judges for frequent adjournments, reducing government litigation, compulsory use of mediation and other alternate dispute resolution mechanism will reduce the workload of judiciary. Delay is also due to the growth of a culture that has made delays acceptable. Reserving a judgment for years and not delivering it after it has been written by a judge also delays the process of justice. SC called the Union government *'Kumbhakaran'* who loved to sleep for long periods but is oblivious of own delay.

Inordinate delay is not only in disposal of court cases but also in the disposal of mercy petitions. In an unprecedented judgment in 2014, SC freed 15 condemned prisoners on grounds of "inordinate, undue and unexplained" delay and "non-consideration of their mental illness" in the disposal of their mercy pleas by the President.

The position of vacancies in all courts is also alarming. As of December 2015, the vacancies in 15,000 subordinate courts across the country stood at 5,111 (21%) against the sanctioned strength of 21,303 judges. In the 24 HCs there were 464 judicial posts vacant (43%) against the sanctioned strength of 1,079.

For swift disposal of cases more of modern technology, performance appraisal and case management systems will further increase efficiency, infuse objectivity and standardisation. It also requires appointment of more judges. Judge-to-population ratio in 2019 was 20.39 judges per million people against developed countries norm of 100. Working hours and working days can also be increased as suggested by RM Lodha, former CJI. System of long court vacations needs introspection. All this can dramatically reduce the backlog. Infrastructural deficiencies and shortage of courts have generally been blamed for delay but non-adherence to problem of procedural timeframe is contributing more to the piling up of cases.

Reforms in judicial system need finances. Central government allocated rupees 5,000 crore for judicial infrastructure and new courts under the 13th Finance Commission but the state governments failed to utilise up to 80% of funds allocated. Annual budgetary allocation requires a leap to rupees 32,000 crores per year which is negligible as compared to large scale farm waivers and huge subsidies. Political parties are more concerned with populist measures rather than reforms in judicial system or even health and education sectors as they are not vote catchers.

As a liberal democracy, we must have well enforced fewer but critical rules for effective governance. We have more than sufficient laws for attending to misdeeds and sincere and effective implementation is more relevant than further legislation. Jain Commission in its "Report of the Commission on Review of Administrative Laws" rightly pointed out that multiplicity and complexity of laws and rules hampers growth and facilitates corruption. About 1,300 central laws and several thousand state laws need repealing, rationalisation and simplification but progress has been pathetically slow. We also need transparency of court proceedings, judicial accountability, increase in judge-population ratio, time-bound filling of vacant posts, and transparency in appointments, promotion and transfer of judges.

Judges must refrain from accepting frivolous Public Interest Litigations (PILs). Centre and states account for nearly 70% of cases in courts which needs to be checked. Fast track courts were established in 2001 and they have disposed of 85% of cases assigned to them but the scheme was discontinued in March 2011. Government's proposal to have fast track courts for deciding cases against MPs and MLAs has been rejected by the Supreme Court on the ground that law should treat all citizens equally.

Law on contempt of court has been a subject of sharp criticism as judiciary is not above law in a democracy. As human beings, judges are also susceptible to err and mere criticism of a judgment or a judge does not constitute sufficient ground for invocation of the dreaded law. On this Markandey Katju remarked that in a democracy people are supreme and all authorities, including President or Prime Minister, are servants of the people who have a right to criticise judges. Fali Nariman described it as "dog's law". On heavy criticism of some decisions in the UK, Lord Denning said, "We do not fear criticism, nor do we resent it."

In a democracy, judiciary is the basis of delivery of justice and police is to implement legal system, book the errant and investigate cases for judiciary to deal with. Speedy justice requires a combination of administrative action, police investigation and judicial judgment.

Police department in India needs tremendous reforms. As against sanctioned strength of 20.8 lakh in December 2011, all states and UTs had 4.2 lakh vacancies. Poor population-linked ratio of policemen needs improvement. Against a UN norm of 222 police personnel per lakh of population, India's officially sanctioned strength is a paltry 181, and the actual strength is an abysmal 137. There are also enormous shortfalls in the number of police *'chowkis'*, weapons, forensic science laboratories and the like. Nearly a million items sent for forensic examination, a shocking 38% remain unattended for a year or more. All these result in low conviction rate which is 47%, as compared to more than 85% in developed democracies.

In India there is undue police attention for VIPs at the cost of ordinary people. In a democracy the idea that some people are special is admittedly offensive. As against 84 officially designated VIPs in Britain, 125 in Japan and 252 in US, India has 5,79,092. India's police-to-population ratio is one cop for 663 citizens while it is 1810 cops for the same number of VIPs. Rashtrapati Bhawan best symbolises the VVIP obsession of police force and its VIP culture. There is one Joint Commissioner, one DCP, 10 ACPs, 20 Inspectors and another 1,000 men in Rashtrapati Bhawan besides 200 ITBP personnel and President's Bodyguard. On the other hand, only one Joint Commissioner heads the entire Northern Range of Delhi with population of over 75 lakh. Nobody can deny security importance for VIPs in a country targeted by terrorist and Naxalite violence but police deployment for VIPs far exceeds need and police security has become a status symbol. Supreme Court has repeatedly stressed the need to trim police cover for VIPs.

Police reforms are urgent to ensure functional independence of men in uniform, their insulation against political intimidation, arbitrary transfer and insecurity of tenure, and poor pay and service conditions. Similarly, low police-to-population ratio, besides obsolete policing practices, needs urgent reforming. Supreme Court gave a historic judgment on September 22, 2006 directing state governments to set up three new institutions: State Security Commission to insulate police from extraneous pressures, Police Establishment Board to give autonomy to police in personnel matters, and Complaints Authorities to ensure greater accountability by the police. SC also suggested minimum tenure of two years for the police chief and officers on operational duties, separating investigation and law and order functions, and several other steps to insulate police from political interference in discharging their day-to-day duties. According to our Constitution, police is a state subject and it is the states' responsibility to legislate on issues concerning law and order. In December 2006, SC directed the states to de-politicise the police forces to ensure that they may discharge their responsibilities in accordance with the law of the land rather than act at the behest of the politicians. Democratic structure may itself collapse if police are not able to take lawful action against certain categories of criminals just because they have political clout. Similarly, inability of police to act against gangsters and agitators taking shelter behind children and women is adding to increase in lawlessness. Politicians devoid of national interests are the root cause of these problems.

In another judgment Supreme Court said, "Reforms are not happening due to states' cussedness. Chief Ministers treat the police department as their *zamindari* (fiefdom). They are against reforms because they don't want to give policemen autonomy." Model Police Act submitted by an expert committee suggesting creation of state police boards for deciding on promotions and transfer of cops, ensuring fixed tenure of police chiefs and other key functionaries, earmarking dedicated personnel for crime investigation and improved service conditions of policemen failed to be tabled in the Parliament. Policemen also need to undergo attitudinal transformation and skill development.

Police reforms will improve governance, make it more accountable and create an environment where police consider upholding rule of law as its paramount duty. Their core values must be based on integrity, rule of law, respect for human rights and accountability to citizens. Police is not a service but a calling. Modernising police recruitment and training, developing technological skills, and improving the abysmal working and living conditions of subordinate police personnel are urgent needs.

Central Bureau of Investigation (CBI) is another significant democratic institution that safeguards democracy. It was constituted in 1963 by Ministry of Home Affairs as a police force under Delhi Special Police Establishment Act, 1946. It is an agency to investigate crimes, arrest suspects and file charge sheets. Earlier, by a directive, known as 'Single Directive', CBI was barred from initiating a probe against a senior officer of the rank of joint secretary and above without the prior permission of the government. After years of legal wrangling and see-saw battle between legislature and judiciary, a Supreme Court constitutional bench struck down the Single Directive in May 2014 giving CBI freedom to proceed against senior bureaucrats of the rank of joint secretary and above found involved in corruption cases.

Unfortunately, CBI does not have a very healthy reputation for being scrupulously honest and independent, and has been freely manipulated by its political masters. In a tongue-lashing comment during its investigation into the coal scam, SC dubbed CBI as "caged parrot" speaking in its master's (Centre's) voice for being meek and subservient to political bosses. SC has called Intelligence Bureau (IB) as a 'chicken' and these remarks have belittled the two prime investigating institutions. CBI often succumbs to the pressure of political leaders and this is a cause for serious concern. The normal perception is that investigating agencies, both at Centre and state levels, are usually hand-in-glove with the ruling party and vulnerable to high-level interference. It is termed as 'private militia' of the government and the charge of its hounding the opposition cannot be taken lightly. A former CBI director, US Misra, remarked, "The fact remains, I won't hide it, that when we investigate cases against prominent political leaders, there are some influences to keep the progress report pending or present it in a certain way." He cited the examples of BSP chief Mayawati's alleged disproportionate assets and the multi-crore Telgi scam. He said that CBI is a handmaiden of the party in power. Another CBI Chief, Dr. AP Mukherjee, while praising Rajiv Gandhi as a remarkable human being, has revealed in his book, "Unknown Facets of Rajiv Gandhi, Jyoti Basu, Inderjit Gupta" that Rajiv Gandhi wanted commission paid by the suppliers of major defence materials to be utilised "solely for the purpose of meeting the inescapable expenses of the party".

CBI is also not out of the corruption net and SC inflicted the biggest embarrassment on former CBI chief Ranjit Sinha by ordering him in November 2014 to completely keep off from the 2G case as there were prima facie "credible" charges that he had attempted to help the accused in the spectrum scam, and delay prosecution in the Aircel-Maxis case. No CBI chief had ever been indicted by the Supreme Court in such damaging terms.

The manner in which political arms controlled the strings of investigation by CBI and Enforcement Directorate (ED) in Jain Hawala Case, led SC to comment, "This experience revealed to us the need for insulation of these agencies from any extraneous influences." CBI must be made truly autonomous like Election Commission by insulating it from executive influence. It may be made accountable to a bipartisan committee of Parliament rather than to government in power. The CBI chief should be selected by a collegium which may include the Prime Minister, leader of opposition in the Parliament, CJI and others. CBI must cultivate its own cadre of officers drawn from a wide pool of talent, and be given its own budget.

Though maintenance of law and order is the responsibility of the state, it is the prime duty of citizens to observe the rules judiciously and avoid their violation. In India, we take pride in violation of rules and laws of the land with immunity. Time has come when all of us must rise above our limited perception and cultivate a culture for respect of law. A 'fearless' society is the pride of true democracy, a society without fear of authority is an invitation to anarchy. The path of democracy will continue to remain thorny and can never be smooth unless people learn to respect law and vital police and judicial reforms are implemented.

Media, the fourth pillar of a democratic system, is the conscience keeper of the society and tracks transparency in the other three systems viz. legislative, executive and judiciary. It has to play a more responsible role to keep constant vigil on the government and the suspicious functionaries. It must expose any scam or nexus between bureaucrats, politicians and industry and force the government to take appropriate action. It has to constantly shake the slumbering system from falling in deep sleep. It must also not allow the government to initiate regressive and draconian laws that are against the spirit of democracy and the constitutional rights of the people. However, media must break free of the shackles of biases and safeguard itself against regression and falling into the trap of vested social and political interests. It must report events, incidents and views truthfully and honestly leaving no scope for favour or prejudice. It has to be transparent for the growth of democracy and welfare of the masses. A healthy and unbiased professional relationship, not a relationship of hostility or intimacy, between politicians and media is the requisite of a free society for the growth of democracy. Journalists are tempted to get closer to politicians for selfish motives and that is fundamentally inconsistent with their assigned task of presenting an honest picture of facts. Politicians are mostly unable to read the media correctly, while the media reads the politicians slightly better. British MP, Enoch Powell aptly remarked, "For a politician to complain about media is like a ship's captain complaining about the sea."

Journalists are probably the most insecure people on the planet and are subjected to all kinds of pressures from authorities, institutions, governments and corporates. Governments muzzle media by denying it advertisements, the main source of their income, and misuse taxpayers' money to pressurise or influence media critical of them. This 'soft censorship' is pervasive but less noticed than direct attack on freedom of press and assault on journalists. Some private sector companies also try to influence news coverage by using similar intimidatory tactics and by withdrawing advertisements. This policy has given rise to committed journalism and *'godi'* (lap) media. It is unfortunate that today 'designer' journalists are increasing for the allurement of money and other favours and are presenting biased and prejudicial views about the government, some politicians or other organisations thus harming the healthy growth of democracy. Their "shops" will soon close as the electorate is now becoming more aware of their real designs.

Development of "committed media" is gaining ground globally and has to be curbed by intelligentsia. Foreign media, with the active support of disgruntled wide cross-section of civil society, is progressively criticising India's national policies. Champions of foreign media adopt double standard. They keep a hawk eye on the biased human rights violations in India but are blind to even serious violations in their own land. The 2019 Democracy Index Report ranked India at the 51st spot and has placed it in the category of 'flawed democracies'. The erosion of civil liberties has been attributed to abrogation of Article 370, repealing Article 55A and removing the special status of JK, and Citizenship (Amendment) Act (CAA) and related initiatives such as National Register of Citizens (NRC). The ranking is evidently biased and an interference in the internal policies of the country. Factually, NRC contained record of legal Indian citizens as per the Citizenship Act, 1955 for Assam, a border state with unique problem of illegal immigrants. Census report of 1961 reported 2.20 lakh illegally entered Assam out of which 1.79 lakh were deported by 1966 but 40 thousand still remained. By the end of December 2017 there were 1.4 crore missing in the NRC report out of 3.3 crore applicants. They are presumed to be illegal immigrants. Internal disruptive forces, unsettled international borders and constant influx of illegal migration are endangering the internal security of the country. Our blinkered political parties joined the media and exploited the Muslim minorities creating an unfounded suspicion in their minds that it is biased against the minorities and all Muslims will be deported. This was all due to narrow and short-term sectarian and regional gains, and dirty vote-bank politics.

Freedom of speech and expression is a significant right in any democracy. This right has always been under great stress in India, a land of great sensibilities, on account of diverse socio-economic, political and cultural realities. Additionally, human beings anywhere in the world cannot be expected to conform to identical views and values. Article 19(1)(a) of the Constitution protects the freedom of speech and expression but Article 19(2) imposes reasonable restrictions against its abuse, including decency, morality and defamation. Every Indian citizen, irrespective of political or idcological leaning, is within his/her constitutional rights to freely articulate a viewpoint within the confines of reasonable restrictions and laws.

Free speech right is nowhere near absolute. The First Amendment to the Constitution was piloted on May 10, 1951 and it imposed "reasonable restrictions" on freedom of expression to protect "the sovereignty and integrity of India, the security of the State, friendly relations with foreign States, public order, decency or morality or in relation to contempt of court, defamation or incitement to an offence." Courts have also protected the right to free speech through many landmark judgments but have also reinforced boundaries. In February, 2012, the Supreme Court gave one of the finest discourses on the virtues of free speech. It said, "Freedom of speech is the bulwark of the democratic process. Freedom of speech and expression is regarded as the first condition of liberty…It has been said that it is the mother of all liberties."

Right to freedom of speech and expression is one of the strongest pillars of democracy but also dangerous for its collapse. Right to freedom of one should never impinge upon the right of the other. It is this fact when ignored weakens democracy. Human Right Activists should not turn blind eye to the right of one for unreasonably supporting the right of the other. For the survival of democracy in India and anywhere in the world, thinkers will have to carefully ponder over the thorny issue of right to speech and expression. Freedom of press is also being misused by TV channels for better Television Rating Point (TRP). Internet and social media spread fake news and poison the views of the people against the integrity of the nation. Mark Twain aptly remarked, "A lie can travel half way around the world while the truth is putting on its shoes." Fake news spreaders, committed media and disgruntled intelligentsia form a disintegration gang to derail India from its path of democracy. Government is coming out with laws to hold social media Apps responsible for this as they were not adhering to Indian Constitution and Indian laws. In their bid to be 'first' to air news, TV channels sometimes give fake or false news to the viewers. In one classic case a TV channel televised "Breaking News" of the death of Pranab Mukherjee when he was admitted in the hospital and then easily got out by tendering an apology.

There is always a thin line between perfect and legitimate freedom of speech and there is difference where the line should be drawn. Freedom without responsibility would lead to anarchy. Most of the important statutory provisions under the ambit of Article 19(2) are detailed in Sections 153A, 295 and 295A of the Indian Penal Code. They deal with hate speech flaming enmity between different groups on grounds like religion and race, defilement of a place of worship or an object held sacred, with intent to insult a religion and blasphemy which is outraging religious feelings. The Supreme Court observed in one of its judgments, "…the freedom has to be guarded against becoming a licence for vilification and condemnation of the government established by law…" Absolute freedom of speech and expression can never be granted, neither in India nor anywhere in the world. It is one of the greatest dangers to the survival and prosperity of democracy everywhere but particularly in India, land of vast diversities.

Application of laws for the powerful and weak is extremely arbitrary and discriminatory. Section 66A of the Information Technology Act was indiscriminately used by police to arrest persons for posting criticism of government and political leaders. A politician could make a false, insulting or foul-mouthed statement with no consequences, but people were arrested for drawing cartoons lampooning Parliament and the Indian Constitution, and arresting even an XI class girl student for posting 'objectionable' comment attributed to a party leader. Examples are endless. In March 2015, the Supreme Court struck down this Section as unconstitutional. It said, "when it comes to democracy, liberty of thought and expression is a cardinal value that is of paramount significance under our constitutional scheme." According to Robert Jackson, the late US Supreme Court Judge, "It is not the function of our government to keep the citizen from falling into error; it is the function of the citizen to keep the government from falling into error." In a totalitarian regime, states are never wrong, only people are, while in democracy the reverse is the truth.

Freedom of expression is the foundation of a liberal democracy but books, films, plays etc. have been often banned in India under social pressure by weak governments. Perumal Murugan, a leading Tamil writer had to declare him 'dead', withdraw his controversial novel '*Mathorupaagan*' and all his works under pressure of some caste organisations in Tamil Nadu, and vowed not to write anymore. Numerous other books have been banned, some in the whole country and some only in some states. All through history there have been famous exiled writers like Dante, Voltaire, Victor Hugo and artists like Picasso and Dali, and many intellectuals who left South Africa during the apartheid years.

Same is the fate of films and plays. One Bollywood film was banned in one Hindi speaking state while two other neighbouring states in the same linguistic region made it tax free. This shows that cultural differences do not crop up in different linguistic regions but can emerge even in the same linguistic belt. "*Fatwa*" was issued against three Kashmiri girls for being part of a rock band which they performed in Srinagar. History has been a major casualty distorted and viewed from widely different perspectives.

Perennially anxious about upsetting their vote banks, politicians are the first ones to raise a war-cry against thinkers and artists. Instead of protecting the victims, the government fears a small violent mob and maintaining law and order is only an excuse to bow down before the anti-democratic elements that are swelling. It shamelessly surrenders to a belligerent few who are enemies of open society. Bowing to threats is a sign of opportunism not wisdom. Protecting rights of writers and artists is a bedrock principle of liberal democracy. The problem is not that majorities are getting more intolerant; the problem is that no one is willing to stand up to small disruptive groups that can hold values hostage. Peaceful protest is a fundamental right of democracy but not unjustified violent protests. Any agitating or vociferous group with a bit of political clout or nuisance value can hold freedom of millions to ransom. Wendy Doniger writes in 'The Hindus: An alternative History', "We can learn from India's long and complex history of pluralism not just of the pitfalls to avoid but the successes to emulate." She suggests that we follow the paths of Ashoka, Harsha, Akbar, Kabir or Gandhi and urges us to take lessons from the *Bhakti* movement, which advocated a theology of love rejecting hierarchy and violence. In ancient India various versions of the holiest of epics like the *Ramayan* and *Mahabharat* were created and celebrated. Everyone had a right to find his own truth. Stopping free flow of ideas is against India's innate culture. Belief that harmony makes small things grow and lack of it makes great things decay, has been fundamental to the survival and prosperity of all cultures and religions that migrated to India.

Invasion of private lives and personal choices of social life of the people is on the rise. Prohibition and ban on food products are not justified. The courts have also upheld that meat ban is "unreasonable, arbitrary and discriminatory restriction that violates the fundamental rights." Bans on beauty contests, celebrating Valentine's Day, wearing jeans and carrying mobiles by girls etc. are ridiculous and more than irritants. Lynching due to consensus marriage of couples from two different religions or communities is a heinous crime and needs severe punishment for the culprits. A democratic country requires respectful accommodation of differences. As a modern nation, we must 'ban the bans'. However, forced religious conversion on allurement of marriage, job or money must be banned by law.

Religious fundamentalists are exploiting sentiments of innocent people and even school and college going adolescents to poison their minds. Liberal India has gradually given way to the unruly mob. Censorship is being handed over to the violent minority. We fail victims of mob-violence again and again but the state must give the mob no quarter. Vote-bank politics is also pushing some parties to inciting the communal feelings of certain sections of the society. Unfortunately, the extreme often tends to get noticed far more easily but if moderate and more reasonable voices are sparked into alertness and participation, the more extreme ones will automatically be pushed back and finally silenced.

Strength of any democracy depends on the strength of the pillars on which it rests. Indian Constitution provided for very strong pillars bur with the passage of time the democratic institutions started weakening due to lack of political will and greedy vote-bank politics. Pitfalls multiplied and the path of democracy became more slippery. The onus to strengthen the pillars and make the path of democracy smooth now rests on formidable public pressure, vibrant judiciary and a strong and determined leadership.

15

DARK TUNNEL AND BEYOND

After independence India had the challenge to accomplish economic, social, political and institutional transitions simultaneously but miserably faltered on all four. Economic growth is the essence of progress of democracy and if it falters, political and social transitions can be fatal. Four forces blocked the path of economic growth. They were, faulty policies and short-sightedness of power-drunk ruling party, lack of courage of timid economists, greed of big business houses with no concern to create a pro-business environment, and turning blind eye to welfare schemes due to vote-bank politics.

The second force of transition was social. This force is most challenging and has huge bearing on economic growth also. Vast growing middle class, the most formidable section of society, and powerless poor were completely neglected. Focus was only on wealthy who had no interest in the growth and welfare of the masses.

Besides the poor and the middle class, women were also marginalised which hugely damaged prospects of social growth for this large section of society. Social slide continued for over seven decades and no efforts were made to narrow the gulf between rich and poor, and educated and uneducated. A democratic system has to ensure that social development is in tune with democratic values and norms requiring social stability and opportunities for equitable development for all sections of society, particularly the poor and down trodden.

The third force of transition was political that cannot flourish without economic and social democracy. Corruption is the greatest stumbling block of this formidable institution that not only damages the smooth democratic path but also strangulates economic and social growth. Corruption and scams increased with the passage of time and political parties remained busy filling their own pockets. No efforts were made to create strong and effective institutions like Lokpal to eradicate political corruption.

The fourth hurdle against growth was absence of institutional reforms. All political parties, at least formally, talked about administrative reforms and more participatory governance but failed to take any concrete steps to achieve them. Their policies encouraged plutocracy, government by the wealthy that damaged the basic institutions of democracy. William Bryan Jennings has put the matter perfectly, "Plutocracy is abhorrent to a republic; it is more despotic than a monarchy, more heartless than an aristocracy, more selfish than a bureaucracy." National parties like NDA and UPA have shown no commitment to drive institutional reforms needed for good governance. Regional parties lack national vision and Left parties do not believe in market-based outcomes. AAP, with its anti-corruption commitment, could have filled this space but it feels that free water, electricity and food are the only ways to stay in power even at the cost of development.

Democracy will collapse if it falters on any one of the four transitions. India has wavered on the four transitions not because the democracy is flawed but due to wrong choice of economic policies, endemic corruption, poor governance, cheap vote-bank politics, corrupt bureaucratic model of governance, and a lumbering law enforcing system. India has lived in a very repressive regime, got democracy served on a silver plate, and did not earn it by effort or sacrifice. Anything earned easily is respected least and because of this, it is failing to achieve what it could and should have achieved. A repressed society cannot be creative and our vibrant but chaotic democracy has been steadily declining.

Two sets of forces affected the growth of Indian democracy. First is of geographical and historical forces of the past that is not amenable to change. Geography divided India into diversified states that have tendency to weaken the federal structure of democracy. Geography also created military dictatorship, communist, terrorist sponsored, or fragile democracies as India's hostile neighbours that are always threatening its existence. Historically, India has assimilated various religions, cultures, castes and languages in its fold for centuries that have created diversities not easy to change. Indian democracy has to strive, thrive and struggle to prosper amidst all these historical and geographical creations.

Second set of forces likely to damage the growth of our vibrant democracy is self-created after independence. Freedom came to India without much struggle. Physically we became independent but mentally continued with the slavish mentality of centuries. It created a culture of greed and grabbing that made us more self-centred and we viewed our nation as fragments and not as a unified whole. We lived under the rule of rod and rule of law was alien to our nature. We are a democratic nation but deep down in thought and action we continue to be undemocratic. The philosophy of democracy has never been in our blood and never a way of our life. We need to create a culture of respect for democracy. We always think what country can do for us and not what we can do for the country. Our leaders, efficient in creating chaos, agitations and '*dharnas*' before independence are still following the same to stay in power. They continue to follow the same negative brand of politics, propagating government of the goons, by the goons and for the goons. The colonial masters followed the policy of 'divide-and-rule' and wanted to keep the masses illiterate for their political gain. The masters of today have blindly continued with the same legacy. All these factors, coupled with political and social corruption, weak law enforcing system, intolerant religious and social fanatics, disintegration gangs, greedy and biased media, and disruptive foreign media, have put Indian democracy under great threat and are constantly damaging its growth and even survival.

There have been rays of hope but reforms have moved at snail's pace due to political cowardice, intellectual myopia and policy paralysis. A healthy democracy needs a vibrant economy but India's economic development during the last seven decades suffered badly. India is now in need of serious reforms to strengthen business environment. Job creation and productivity gains are the most powerful forces for improving living standards. If weak economic performance continues, a large part of our population will remain trapped in poverty. India is a place difficult to do smooth, stable and progressive business. We have to create opportunities for business with manufacturing and labour-rich services, raise farm productivity and efficiency of distribution, and increase public spending on basic services. These forces will set off a cycle generating more revenues, enabling meeting of funding needs for social development. Today voter preference is social and economic development. He wants empowering access to education, health, infrastructure and jobs, else millions of youth will fall prey to the lure of extremism, crime and violence. Incremental changes will not catapult India to a robust economy. Tough decisions are required for long-term economic health even if they inflict short-term pain. All hesitations and frictions must be overcome and wheels of economy freed from the mud and sand that retard its racing.

Democracy may be the preferred form of government, but it is not guaranteed to produce liberal outcomes unless it revolves around economic empowerment and functions like a welfare ladder. It is essential that everyone must ascend that ladder but the deprived, underprivileged and those at the lower rung of the ladder must rise at twice the pace of elites.

Socially, India is one of the most divided countries on account of religions, castes, creeds, classes, languages and regional disparities. To perpetuate these divisions and to keep them in power, the political leaders not only maintained these divisions created by history and our colonial masters but further widened them. This suited their political gains and vote-bank diplomacy. Policy of appeasement of minorities followed by the short-sighted disgruntled politicians further sharpened the diversities that derailed the smooth functioning of democracy. It is not democracy that is at fault but lack of cohesion among the socio-political forces moving in anti-national directions that impede its growth and make it a flawed democracy. India needs to make an ideological shift from the colonial thinking of social and economic divisions to human resource management and poverty alleviation.

Politically, democratic institutions have been vastly corroded and their health and growth damaged. Credibility of Parliament, the most sacred political institution, has woefully declined and needs to change its culture. It cannot function fruitfully unless structural fault lines in its functioning are resolved. Election financing is the most corrupt area of our political system. To check dubious political funding and corruption in political financing, political parties must be regarded as "public authority" and brought under RTI domain. With no constructive common policies, the political parties are contributing to the retardation of the nation rather than to its acceleration. In the absence of political reforms, Indian democracy will continue to remain fractured, limping, falling and struggling to rise.

Democratic institutions in India need to be strengthened. Unfortunately, slavish mentality of centuries has chained us to orthodoxy and made us impervious to accept change. Any change, howsoever progressive, is resisted by the uncompromising and destructive opposition. Forces of disintegration immediately join hand, add fuel to the fire, resulting in violence and large-scale destructions to resist the change. History bears testimony to the fact that stagnant systems not amenable to change crumble under their own weight. We must realise that change is the fundamental principle of nature and must change our negative culture of fear of change. To make a new 'Shining India' we require big ideas, decisive leadership, a happy coincidence of circumstances, incremental implementation of change, and above all a will to accept the change.

Community is a formidable agent of change. It can play a significant role in keeping a check on the elected bodies and the corrupt political system. We cannot rely on conventional means for reform. People must lead massive social movements against corrupt political systems rather than just leave them to civil society organisations. Mass social movements will make our hard-boiled politicians realise that if they do not reform, they will perish. Change from within the culture is slow and normally vehemently resisted. We need revolutionary crusade on a large scale as sustained mass movements are genesis of progress and path-breaking reforms in a society. Small ripples become waves and waves turn into a tsunami. People have to rise, jolt and wake the slumbering governments. They must create a sense of fear among the corrupt politicians that they will be rooted out if they work against the interests of the nation. Strict and enforceable anti-corruption laws with a strong Lokpal are essential. Bureaucratic system also needs to be jolted from its deep slumber to make it realise that the society cannot take things for granted. People need action and not hollow promises. People must wake up, rise, and "stop not till the goal is achieved."

Judiciary is another vital constitutional body to keep a check on the corrupt political institutions. It is an irony that in democracy elected bodies are corrupt and unelected bodies like Supreme Court, Election Commission,

Comptroller and Auditor General and armed forces are most respected and generally free from corruption. The legitimacy of the elected politicians is temporary given for a few years by the voters and withdrawable for non-performance. It is court, the non-elected body, that determines the political guilt with total disregard to status and power of the guilty. It keeps a check on the elected government to follow constitutional tracks and judiciously implement rule of law that is most vulnerable to political pressure. In the discharge of its duties it is under constant threat. Judges are under great stress and recuse from taking controversial decisions particularly those related to social issues or concerning religions and religious practices. Biased Human Rights Activists who fall a victim to the pressure of violent mobs for right to freedom of speech and expression ignoring similar rights for others are further threatening judicial system. A strong and unfettered judiciary not amenable to bend or break under any pressure is the sure hope for the survival and growth of our democracy. We need strong political will to overhaul the criminal justice delivery system and dynamism to implement judicial and police reforms for the growth and survival of our democracy.

There is now shift in the orientation of media also. Earlier, it strove to represent the ideals of democracy and created a culture that emphasised rationality and logic. Committed media has now taken over neutral and unbiased journalism for self-interest, lure of money and better future prospects in the corrupt political system.

Fake news that spread like wild fire has become an integral part of social media resulting in poisoning the views and minds of the people. Public pressure against greedy and committed journalism will force the biased media to change its culture of favouritism and self-interest.

India is capable of doing a lot but does not do half the things due to its culture of *'chalta hai'*. The attitude of band-aid and patchwork in governance must be vehemently broken. Being by nature a tolerant society, we often come to terms with the inefficiency of the corrupt systems of government. Change is happening but only in micro steps. We must further strengthen this change, make it a more enduring reality and restore confidence in existing institutions of democracy.

Besides the fast growing political, social and economic problems, religious fundamentalism and communalism have acquired dangerous forms and alarming proposition in India, a land of many religions, communities, traditions and cultures. They are a great threat to the survival of democracy not only in our multi-religious country but all over the world. Religious fundamentalism acts as an ideology which advocates orthodoxy and strict compliance to the fundamental tenants of religion. It vehemently opposes progressive reforms in order to establish its exclusive control on the respective communities. Communalism is an affront to India's nationalist identity and a tragic setback to its evolving secular culture. It is subversive of our democratic political stability and destroyer of our glorious heritage of harmony and composite culture.

Multiple diversities in India have given rise to polarisation that has strengthened disintegration gangs. International forces are providing moral and financial support to these gangs to weaken India as a strong and robust emerging economy and tearing apart the fabric of democracy. An established democracy in a country need not be attacked from outside now. Forces damaging its demography and culture need to be inflamed to annihilate its existence. These gangs are now adopting similar nefarious methods in India. They are advocating the dangerous strategy of attacking educational institutions to brainwash children in their mid-teens to destroy the tolerant culture of India. The world is moving towards progress and liberalism and these youths in their impressionable age are being dragged towards ignorance, irrationality and fanaticism.

Indian democracy is now assuming shades of acentric majoritarianism that are stealing the freedom of silent and tolerant majority. Brute forces of intolerance are encouraging diversities and trying to strangulate the democratic forces. Mobilisation and mass movements, once considered the foundations of a strong social change, are now pressurising governments for unbridled freedom. Corrupt political parties, instead of checking corruption in their home, resort to *dharnas* to support their corrupt leaders. Road blocks are adding to the woes of the disciplined citizens and depriving them even of their right to free movement, not to talk of right to life. The democratic right to assemble has increasingly become a means for small disgruntled groups to curb freedom of the disciplined majority. Unfortunately, everyone demands his rights unmindful of sacrificing the rights of others resulting in subversion of the core values of democratic principles. Governments tend to abdicate responsibility, even when faced with a handful of cynical violent mob that gags the disciplined and peaceful majority. Responsibility to check destructive impulses of violent minorities impinging upon the autonomy of vast and disciplined silent majority now falls on the courts. Exercising freedom of expression to suppress freedom of expression of others and use it for violence, communal discord and national disintegration should be severely dealt with. India can be a super power but for these damaging forces. We have to see whether we want unlimited democracy and limited development or limited democracy and unlimited development.

Peace and harmony prevail when a nation celebrates pluralism, promotes tolerance and goodwill among diverse communities, and when we purge the toxin of hatred, envy, jealousy and aggression from our everyday lives, says Pranab Mukherjee. He also says that people are happier in countries where personal freedom is guaranteed, democracy is secure and regardless of their economic condition, citizens are happy in a climate of peace. To maintain peace and stability in the society and strengthen tolerance, religious worship should be a matter of personal faith, confined to homes and designated places of worship. The sanctity of religion should not be spilled on the dirt of the streets and filth of the roads. Fortunately, centuries old Indian culture of *Vasudhaiva Kutumbakam'* and civilisational ethos of tolerance have weakened diversities and must be further strengthened for the growth of a healthy and vibrant democracy. Indian democracy is strong, robust and stable with tolerance as its core principle but tolerant majority must stand against the intolerant minority and resist the forces of intolerance. At a time when India stands at a growing divide between religious fundamentalism and tolerance we must remember what Gandhi stood for.

It is a tragedy that India has never learnt from history and slowly and slowly got consumed in it. During the last over thousand years, India has never presented a unified defence against invaders that resulted in the steady squeezing of its geography. It is not that the invaders were strong; it is that Indian rulers, even if strong, were never united against the invaders considering it to be the problem of the state that faced them. Greed made them fall in the clutches of those invaders who soon devoured them also. Regarding danger to independence, Ambedkar aptly remarked, "She lost it by the infidelity and treachery of some of her own people..." Same story continues even today. There is less fear from any foreign invasion but more from the enemies at home. A frustrated brother at home is always more dangerous than even a strong outside enemy. A splintered majority, howsoever large, cannot succeed against even a small unified minority. Democracy in India will be under constant threat unless people learn to offer unified resistance against the forces of intolerance and disintegration, both internal and external.

Indian democracy today is boisterous and factionalised with a variety of conflicting socio-political groups all pulling in divergent directions. With that magnitude of divergence, it is sometimes called a flawed democracy. But this flaw is its beauty also that cannot be appreciated by totalitarian states that believe in "Bullet over ballot". Unfortunately, our elected representatives have let us down through sloth and corruption, and democratic institutions have failed to provide social and economic equality, particularly to women and down-trodden. India is said to be an open society with a closed mind.

It is not only in India that democracy is struggling to flourish. With the passage of time democracy all over the world has undergone a sea-change even though the basic structure has remained the same. Earlier democracies worked within a tight set of rules and a comprehensive system of checks and balances, and harmony between legislature, executive and judiciary, with strength to test them in dynamic situations. Today, democracy is 'hot' where impatience is strong and people matter more than issues. Democracy and freedom have long been considered conjoined twins but now "we want freedom" gang is forcing their separation. Intellectual myopia has blinded the short-sighted leaders with rabid behaviour trying to foment divisions based on religion, race and ethnicity. Idealism is being replaced by emotions, and unidentified and unjustified demands matter most. The flame of democracy needs to be protected from the storm of damage of these regressive forces. Mahatma Gandhi aptly remarked, "Democracy disciplined and enlightened is the finest thing in the world. Democracy prejudiced, ignorant, superstitious will land itself in chaos."

Democracy, by definition, is, government "by the people" which in actual practice is government of the representatives elected by the people. Quality of a government will, therefore, depend on the quality of the elected representatives. People must elect honest representatives else change those divorced from national interests by the power of their franchise. Core of a vibrant democracy is the ethos of the electorate. It is not democracy that is at fault, the problem lies with the 'people' who elect their leaders and the elected leaders who form the government. 'People' created democracy and now only 'People' can save it. Howsoever hard a government may try, the problems facing the country cannot be eradicated or even minimised unless the basic thinking of the 'people' changes. Change is visible though slow and it will take more time to undergo constructive change for our democracy to flourish.

Democracy is vibrant only if our politicians imbibe democratic values and work for the welfare of the nation.

Commitment to party may be essential for them but service to the people and welfare of the nation must always be in their head and heart. Their detachment from national progress will bring democracy to a grinding halt. Challenge is not to change devils into angels but to get even devils to do the right thing.

It is an undisputed truth that no system of government is perfect. Monarchy, fascism, and theocracy are all ruins of the past and now democracy scores over all. In India, democracy has still not matured and continues to struggle. A look at the path of over seven decades of democracy reveals that democracy in India has been tumbling on its path rather than flourish fruitfully. Path laid by the Constitution framers had pitfalls from the very beginning. Very little efforts were made later on to smoothen it and the pitfalls continued to widen due to partisan and greedy vote-bank politics, and lack of far-sighted leaders. Opportunistic politicians are always stroking the smouldering fire to flame the religious, regional and caste passions of the people for their selfish ends. No democracy in the world is free from identity politics of one form or another and India with its vast diversities is also a victim of this virus. The result is that society is getting more fragmented giving way to mobocracy, intolerance and competitive politics. Diversity, instead of becoming a boon, is putting our democracy on the defence. There is decline in morals and values, and constitutional democracy is giving way to money and muscle power. The damsel of democracy will become an object of exploitation in the hands of the criminals unless men and women of integrity join politics, induct moral values and save the nation from the danger of disintegration.

Social systems have been changing in the past and shall continue to change in future also. One system gives birth to another and the process continues. Violence of the people and terror of the monster of authority gave birth to democracy, government of the *demos*. It is now the responsibility of the *demos* to secure, preserve and strengthen democracy. If the elected representatives are corrupt, and shed their moral and ethical values, if the *demos* are intolerant beyond limit, if the *demos* demand limitless liberties, the *demos* will give birth to the monster of authority to devour democracy and another system will be born out of democracy again giving rise to terror and autocracy. The cycle will go on till eternity.

Democracy everywhere has its problems but no system better then democracy has so far been conceived. India is a crisis in search of a solution. The people alone can provide this and stop this cycle of upheavals if they learn to live with peace and tolerance. Danger to the smooth working and consequent survival of democracy varies from country to country and nation to nation. India is infested with marked rise in polarisation and dangerous divisive forces absent in most other countries. Difference of opinions and ideas is the basic part of human nature but forces within and outside, are exploiting disparities to weaken democracy and break it into fragments. Intolerance of some religions, cultures and regions, not believing in the philosophy of 'live and let live' is threatening the smooth working and growth of Indian democracy. Our effort should be to let diversities converge to a point rather than make them a source of intolerance.

Contrary to the apprehension of many thinkers, democracy in India has successfully survived on the uneven path and will continue to struggle on the uneven, bumpy and slippery path. Some fear "possible collapse of the nation." Solution to any such fear lies in our united stand to raise our voice against the disgruntled forces of disintegration. The irony is that two intellectuals can't stay together but hundred 'fools' can. The intellectual forces must take a unified and solid stand against the forces of diversity and polarisation that raise their monstrous head against the unity of the nation and crush the intolerant regressive forces.

World's largest democracy is at the crossroads. Disparities have given rise to religious intolerance that has encouraged forces of polarisation. Tolerance of all faiths and religions has been the greatest strength of India in the past and shall continue to be in future also. The tragedy is that tolerant majority falls an easy prey to the threats of the intolerant violent minority. Challenges of acute religious intolerance, secularism and threat to federal structure are grave but they collapse before a unified nation. All pillars of democratic system are under assault but pragmatic and implementable solutions need to be explored. Democracy can survive and thrive only if the Constitution is followed in letter and spirit by all sections of the society.

We again stand at another moment of awakening, a pivotal moment of opportunity and a challenge "that comes but rarely in history". We need to make our political system corruption-free that may lead to social and economic growth and make India a tolerant religious, linguistic and regional society built on a new paradigm of wellbeing and trust. Strong democracy delivers peace and prosperity, weak ruins nations. We can't progress with a myopic mind or grow with shallow ideals. Policy inertia must be dumped. India is not stagnant. It is on the path of evolution. It can absorb a limp on the road, but it will not be crippled. A determined nation can never be defeated and as a nation we need will and courage to protect the flame of our sacred democracy. Wheels of change have been set in motion towards a new horizon. We are on the right path. Let us continue our sacred journey and be change bearers and agents of change. Glimmer of light is clearly visible beyond the tunnel but we have many miles to go and many formidable challenges to overcome. Long journeys are covered in short and steady steps. There are rays of hope and amidst the encircling gloom democracy in India will continue to struggle for its survival.

INDEX

C

H

Haksar, PN, on Rao 70

Handerson Report on 1962 conflict 24-25

Health care

    -problems & expenditure 202

    -Modi care 202

Horse-trading 76

Housing & environment

    -air pollution 203

I

Illegal colonies

    -undemocratic 193

Indian Constitution

    -preamble 12

    -fundamental rights 12

    -flexibility 13

    -institutions 14

    -initial pitfalls 15

Indian democracy

    -birth & strength 11

    -problems 100

    -under threat 148

    -pillars 240, 286

    -need of reforms 272-73

Indian Peace Keeping Force (IPKF) 67

Indo-China relations 25-26

Inner-party democracy 172

Institutions in democracy

    -political favours 163

    -SC on governor 163

International Finance Corporation (IFC) 201

Irrationality of thought

    -religious intolerance 232, 285

    -dilutes democracy 234

J

Janta Party 50

Jaswant Singh

    -accompanying terrorists 86

Jawahar *Rozgar Yojna* 62

Jennings, Bryan, on plutocracy 269

Judicial system

    -power to appoint judges 240

    -collegium system 241

    -corruption 241

    -judicial activism 245